COUNTRY COMFORT

The Complete Book
of **Home**
Baking

Monica Musetti-Carlin

Introduction by Chef Christopher Holt

Hatherleigh

COUNTRY COMFORT: THE COMPLETE BOOK OF HOME BAKING

Hatherleigh Press is committed to preserving and protecting the natural resources of the Earth. Environmentally responsible and sustainable practices are embraced within the company's mission statement.

Hatherleigh Press is a member of the Publishers Earth Alliance, committed to preserving and protecting the natural resources of the planet while developing a sustainable business model for the book publishing industry.

This book was edited and designed in the village of Hobart, New York. Hobart is a community that has embraced books and publishing as a component of its livelihood. There are several unique bookstores in the village. For more information, please visit www.hobartbookvillage.com.

Library of Congress Cataloging-in-Publication Data is available.
ISBN: 978-1-57826-419-3

Country Comfort: The Complete Book of Home Baking is available for bulk purchase, special promotions, and premiums. For information on reselling and special purchase opportunities, call 1-800-528-2550 and ask for the Special Sales Manager.

Cover and interior design by Nick Macagnone

Printed in the United States
10 9 8 7 6 5 4 3 2

DISCLAIMER
Any similarities to existing recipes are purely coincidental.

Acknowledgments

This book is dedicated to my son, Matt, who continues to try new foods and relishes my cooking. To all the wonderfully talented foodies who sent me their family favorites. To my sister, Kathy, who has contributed to every one of my books in the *Country Comfort* series either with her own recipes or those of her friends. As always, to Anna Krusinski, for her talent and patience.

Table of Contents

Foreword

and smiled with weepy ... passed on through generations
are cherished and become priceless because of the memories they
carry with them. Perhaps the most special aspects of home cooking
lie in the selection of the finest ingredients and the loving care in its
preparation.

When I relocated to Texas from Brooklyn, New York, many of my favorite foods such as bialys and rugelach were nowhere to be found. After my retirement, the answer to my dilemma became abundantly clear. If the closest store for these foods was 1,500 miles away, I would have to learn to make them fresh myself. I consulted with my mother who inspired me to duplicate the foods from my childhood. Trial and error, no matter how simple the directions, is a process which leads to constant improvement. Becoming an experienced baker requires patience, observation, and creativity. It took me several years to appreciate the subtle differences in how dough behaves, and particularly how it should feel in your hands to get predictable results.

When Monica asked me to contribute to this special cookbook, I jumped at the chance. Sharing a love of baking, and the bonds it can create, Monica has developed a wonderful collection of recipes that have been passed down for generations, along with some original recipes invented by passionate bakers.

Prepare yourself for a journey back to the place where your dreams were born. Remember when your home was filled with the sweet aromas of baked pastries and breads, and how you were amazed by the endless assortment of tasty and gorgeous goods at your local bakery. Those childhood memories will always remain fresh in your mind. Just as music can remind us of our youth, food can reach even deeper into our souls. It can bring us back to family gatherings at the dinner table and remind us of those who brightened our lives but are no longer with us. When we learn to bake the foods we associate with love, we are rewarded with the opportunity to share those warm experiences with our dearest friends and family.

Oftentimes, we are remembered for the blessings we pass on. At my Aunt's funeral 20 years ago, her husband gave a eulogy and spoke of her in endearing terms as a wife, mother, grandmother, and wonderful friend. He ended his speech by pointing out how she made the best noodle pudding, to which many of us nodded in remembrance and smiled with weepy tears. Recipes passed on through generations are cherished and become priceless because of the memories they carry with them. Perhaps the most special aspects of home cooking lie in the selection of the finest ingredients and the loving care in its preparation.

Country Comfort: The Complete Book of Home Baking contains recipes from home bakers who never gave up until the oven yielded a gift from their past. With every baking venture, we learn how to get closer to perfection. The labor of love could not be more exquisitely defined than through the magic of creation in our kitchens.

As you find new recipes to try within this book, let them inspire you to explore the variations from cultures throughout the world to make them your own. If future generations remember you for that tasty creation, perhaps it may be said that your work was done. Remember, this book isn't just about cooking for yourself; your gift to others may also lie between the pages.

—*Harry I. Myers*

Preface
Passing on Traditions Through Food

Whether you're a world-class pastry chef or a novice home cook, everybody bakes at one time or another. Even in today's busy world, there are so many pleasures in taking the time to bake at home. For a start, you have better control over your ingredients. Baking at home enables you to use fresh eggs and butter right from your own refrigerator, along with sustainable and local ingredients. There is no need to read a label to see what is in your pumpkin muffins (page 43)—you already know each ingredient because you baked them. When you bake your own goodies, you never need to worry about questionable fillers, preservatives, or hidden fats. Allergic reactions are no longer a concern when you can mix your own gluten-free flour or tailor your recipe to specific dietary needs. In fact, your biggest problem will be keeping your freshly baked cookies from being eaten before you can fill the kids' lunchboxes.

Another reason that we bake from home is to share the experience with others; to slow down, share stories, and laugh together. Baking with your children or learning cooking secrets from your parents or grandparents enables you to cross generational lines and stay grounded. It is a wonderful experience to discover where your family recipes have come from and which of your relatives created them. Knowing the history of each recipe, you will hold a heightened respect for the baking process, and get even more enjoyment from eating your baked goods. Passing on recipes from one generation to the next maintains a continuum. You have the opportunity to look back into your ancestors' kitchens and know that your Italian great, great-grandma made the same Pizza Rustica (page 109) for her family every Easter. That connectedness bonds you with your past, and your children with their future, enabling us to feel pride in who we are. A little pride goes a long way, contributing to a strong core to draw upon as you proceed through life. This type of connection instills a positive attitude and pride that you can make something special and creative.

Living in America, a "melting pot" of cultures, we are fortunate to have the opportunity to savor baked goods from across the globe. Incorporating French or Italian pastries, Colonial Tea Breads (page 196), and English Meat Pies (page 92) into our everyday lives contributes to delicious creations in the kitchen. We enjoy treats that are mixtures of various cultures: the best of many recipes whose roots stem from immigrants from different countries. Who would have ever thought to put goat cheese on pizza or buffalo chicken on cupcakes? The crisscrossing of cultures makes for really interesting and inventive combinations. It is fun to take a chance, perhaps combining unexpected flavors like the salty and sweet combination of Buffalo Chicken Cupcakes (page 107). It is also fun to try your hand at decorating your own creations for special occasions.

Birthdays, weddings, anniversaries, and holidays bring out wonderful family recipes that are baked with pride, elaborately decorated, and served with love. When my brother's children were young, their Aunt Dee always made them the most stunning birthday cakes, incorporating pop culture icons like Sesame Street's Big Bird or scenes like a gleaming red fire engine. Whatever the child was most interested in for that particular year, Aunt Dee would make a personalized cake to fit the overall party theme. I have always been impressed by her artistic touch in using different colors and textures and the time it took to bake and sculpt the cakes. Today, my niece Christie has carried on her aunt's artistic tradition with her own baked goods made lovingly for my great-nephew Damien's parties. Her latest baking sensation, Cake Pops (page 158), are popular nowadays, and were a big hit at Damien's first birthday party.

Of course, the true baker doesn't only bake for special occasions. Everyday goods such as breads, cakes, pies, and pastries grace many a baker's repertoire. My mother-in-law Mary was an accomplished baker, and I can still recall our anticipation as she served her famous warm Apple Pie (page 149) after dinner. Those memories take me right back to that moment: back to those warm feelings and enticing aromas.

I often return to my favorite memories of experiencing a particular treat. For example, the scent of freshly baked pies reminds me of my days in the third grade, when I would spend hours reading the *Bobb-*

sey Twins books in the living room of my aunt and uncle's Wyoming home, with the birds chirping and the sun shining outside. My mouth would water as I would envision the freshly baked pies that seemed to always be cooling on the windowsill of the Bobbsey kitchen. I now like to cool pies, like the Zenk Farms Crustless Cranberry Pie (page 135), on my own windowsill, and envision my son's face brightening in anticipation of a slice of homemade pie. I encourage you to use the recipes in this book to invite that same homey feeling into your own kitchen. French pastries remind me of the summer that my husband and I spent in Paris, feasting daily on the never-ending choices of sumptuous pastries like the savory Caviar Éclair (page 29) or the sweet Chocolate Cream Puffs (page 173) in the local charcuteries and patisseries throughout the city. Everyone (tourists included) carried straw shopping baskets casually hung over their shoulders, stocked with freshly baked French Bread (page 77), a chunk of cheese, a bottle of wine, and a bottle of Perrier®.

Memories lie at the heart of each individual, weighing and measuring the special moments in our lives, weaving a tapestry of good times with family and friends. Special occasions stand out, and we embrace every detail, right down to what we have eaten that day: that special dish that our mom might have made for us, or the exciting international flavors that our travels have brought us. Savor those moments and call upon them when you are planning your next birthday dinner or holiday celebration. One small memory of biting into a delicious slice of cake can trigger your senses and take you back to all the rest of your happy reminiscences from that same time. Pass those memories along to your children through preparing meals and baking together, and you will find that they will pass them along to their children, and so on, and so on, through future generations.

Introduction

Home cooking, especially baking, is such a wonderful foundation upon which to build family memories. Monica Musetti-Carlin's *Country Comfort: The Complete Book of Home Baking*—and all of her books in the *Country Comfort* series—truly touch upon and embrace this idea.

Baking: the word alone conjures up so many wonderful pictures in one's mind that there are hardly words to describe. Is there anything so deeply soul satisfying as the aroma of freshly baked dishes coming out of the oven? A savory bacon and cheese quiche, molten lasagna, bubbling fruit pies, and fudgy brownies can all magically turn any house into a home.

Even as a professional chef with over 30 years of experience, I still get excited when bread has that perfect crunch and I still love the simple, humble baked potato sprinkled with sea salt, butter, and olive oil. The highest compliment I can ever receive is, "that took me back to my Grandma's house."

At home, my wife and I truly believe that the core of our family starts around our kitchen table. Like most parents, we want our kids to learn, try, and experience all the good things that life has to offer. Talking, sharing, and eating with family and friends are wonderful ways to expose them to many lessons in life. Teaching our kids the basics of good cooking so that they can feed themselves well is a tool that should not be overlooked.

My wife has a wonderful tradition of baking cupcakes for everyone's birthday. The kids love getting a cupcake for breakfast and my wife loves when everyone helps decorate them the night before. When I am baking, I get as giddy as the kids while we wait for our favorite brownies to come out of the oven. When they are finally done, my kids declare me their superhero…pretty high praise from a 7-year-old and twin 5-year-olds. After dessert, my little girl gives me a big chocolaty kiss and tells me that I am the best daddy ever! These are the moments that will forever remain in our hearts, making each day special and offering us opportunities to appreciate what makes life so wonderful.

This is why I really love Monica's books. They offer fantastic recipes and great insight. With some family and friends, you can have countless hours of enjoyment savoring the delicious dishes found within these pages.

—Christopher Holt, Executive Chef, George Martin: The Original (Rockville Centre, New York)

Note to the Reader

As I approached my sixth book in the *Country Comfort* series, *Country Comfort: The Complete Book of Home Baking*, I couldn't help but think nostalgically of all the special occasions when I've enjoyed baked specialties throughout my lifetime. Selecting the recipes for this collection has been a daunting task, because there are so many wonderful delicacies just waiting to be discovered. From sweet cakes and cookies to savory breads and pies, the choices are endless.

I first chose all of my personal favorites, including goodies that I knew how to make as well as new ones that I wanted to learn more about. Then came the old favorites from my friends' family recipe boxes, passed down by their aunties and grannies. Finally, I included a selection of what is popular now: not only trendy treats like cupcakes and artisanal breads, but also several vegan, sugarless, and gluten-free alternatives to old standbys. With the new awareness that we have regarding healthy food choices, I believe this recipe collection should offer something for everyone. You will also find a diverse selection of ethnic dishes, including instructions on how to bake Italian bread to go with Sunday dinner, Indian naan to dip into chickpeas, and bialys from my local Jewish bagel shop when I was a kid growing up in Brooklyn.

Most of the recipes in this book are for cakes, pies, cookies, and breads, and will lean toward sweet offerings. Yet, not having much of a sweet tooth myself, I made sure to also include a smattering of savory baked goods that are perfect for serving at brunch, offering as appetizers, or enjoying at dinner. You will also find several recipes for tea breads, which use less sugar than most other desserts.

As always, I have reached out to my favorite restaurants, chefs, co-workers, friends, family members, and bakery shops in gathering their recipes and the stories behind them. Some contributors have returned after submitting recipes for previous *Country Comfort* cookbooks, and some I am welcoming for the first time to join in the *Country Comfort* family. The result is a wide selection of enticing combinations of flavors reflecting comfort food with the unmistakable taste of home, along with *nouvelle cuisine* including savories reflecting the diverse culture in which we live.

Wherever possible, I have chosen old-fashioned recipes with a healthier, contemporary twist by including fresh and local fruits, vegetables, fish, meats, artisanal cheeses, and hand-picked garden-fresh herbs. Where a recipe might call for preserves, you will also find a recipe to make your own homemade version. Where a gluten-free flour is needed, you will find a recipe for the specific gluten-free ingredients.

Country Comfort: The Complete Book of Home Baking has something for everyone, no matter what your level of experience may be. The wide selection of contributors has produced recipes that appeal to all types of bakers of all degrees of accomplishment. You will find *Country Comfort: The Complete Book of Home Baking* to be an invaluable resource with helpful, easy-to-follow directions just right for you and your family to enjoy for generations to come.

Part I

BREAKFAST AND BRUNCH

BREAKFAST AND BRUNCH

In most homes, breakfast on the go is a common occurrence on weekdays. Rushing to get the kids off to school, and then hopping in the car or catching the train to work, is a familiar scenario. Downtime doesn't come in until you are on your way to work: a brief respite for an hour or so when you will get the chance to enjoy your breakfast—perhaps a freshly baked Blueberry Scone (pages 15 and 17) that you've tucked into your briefcase.

Warm, homemade Applesauce Oatmeal Muffins (page 13) are just the trick for commuting, as well. Quick and easy, muffins are a nourishing "grab and go" breakfast choice. Try wrapping them with strawberry preserves or add in peanut butter for extra protein (page 27). Do you normally eat oatmeal every morning? Put it in your muffin batter for a nice, healthy twist. See what is ready to harvest in your garden and incorporate it into your batter. Herbs such as fresh chives or dill are perfect for creating delicious, savory muffins. Preparing muffins doesn't take much time. Try saving just a few different kinds from each batch, and freeze them to use at your next brunch with friends, when you can set out a variety of muffins in a decorative basket.

A Savory Brunch Ring (page 26) is also perfect for your Sunday brunch, because it can be conveniently served by the slice. Using family mementos like lovely china plates and your heirloom collection of silverware will add a bit of character to your spread. Set out a platter of fresh fruit to have alongside yummy Baked French Toast (page 11) and gooey Cinnamon Rolls (page 9), warm and dripping with vanilla icing. Serve Brooklyn Bialys (page 6) with your homemade jams (page 27) and spreads, set out in brightly colored dishes or crystal pots to make your breakfast or brunch get-together even more memorable.

Mandel Bread Biscotti

Harry Myers *(Lipan, TX)*
Serves 4-6

> This recipe is a classic eastern European biscotti called mandel bread. There are many variations on the flavorings, including chocolate chips, walnuts, and fruit preserve mixtures. I hope this recipe spurs your creativity.

¾ cup sugar
2 eggs
2 teaspoons baking powder
1 pinch of salt
¼ cup orange juice (see note)
¾ cup oil
3 cups flour

6 ounces chocolate chips (you may combine walnuts, raisins, and chips together or individually)
Raspberry preserves (optional)
Brown sugar (optional)

Preheat an oven to 350°F. Mix all of the ingredients well. The batter should be stiff enough to form into two loaves. On a greased baking sheet, form two loaves approximately 4 inches wide and 12 inches long. If desired, thinly spread raspberry or your favorite preserve inside the loaf (do not spread the preserves on the outside of the loaf, or it will burn during baking). Sprinkle brown sugar on top, if desired. Bake for 30 minutes. Remove from the oven, cool for 10 minutes, and leave the oven on. Slice the loaves into ¾-inch slices (use a sharp cutting edge to prevent cracking). Slightly separate each slice, and place back in the oven to bake for 7 to 10 more minutes to achieve a biscuit consistency. The biscotti will be medium-hard, but they will harden as time passes. By the next day, they will have hardened to qualify as a true biscotti.

Depending on your preference, you may omit the orange juice and add 1 teaspoon of almond extract, vanilla, mint, coconut, or any mixture to create a unique flavor.

Breakfast Scones

Pat Hogeboom *(Central Islip, NY)*
Makes about 1 dozen

> Pat is an author, historian, and former teacher who has lived most of her married life in Oakdale, New York. I was reminded by a mutual associate that she also happens to be a wonderful baker. I immediately contacted her for some of her specialties, and, being the incredible person that she is, she sent them to me within hours.
>
> *Story by Monica*

2 cups flour
3 tablespoons baking powder
½ tablespoon salt
2 tablespoons butter
1 cup egg nog
1 teaspoon rum flavoring (optional)
1 cup pecans
1 cup red cherries, chopped
1 cup green cherries, chopped
1 cup vanilla icing

Preheat an oven to 425°F. Combine the dry ingredients, and blend in the butter. Add egg nog and rum flavoring (if desired), and combine well. Then add nuts and chopped cherries. Spray a 9-inch pie plate, and spread the mixture carefully. Using a sharp knife, cut (but do not separate) the wedges, keeping them within the pan. Bake for 12 to 14 minutes. Let cool, and then squeeze the prepared icing over all. Cut carefully to serve in wedges.

Brooklyn Bialys

Harry Meyers *(Lipan, TX)*
Serves 6-8

I was born and raised in East Flatbush in Brooklyn, New York, in 1942. At that time, there were many family-owned bakeries preparing their goods during the late night hours for the morning customers. The bakery front doors were open to keep the stores cool in the summer, and the aroma of bread baking in the ovens permeated the night air. When I moved to rural Texas in 1994, the foods that I took for granted were no longer readily available.

The bialy, one of my favorites, is a mystery to the bakers here in Texas. Several years ago, the notion of baking bread struck me as a departure from my other interests. After making over 1,000 different kinds of breads, rolls, and pastries, my wife and I tried making bialys.

Baking bread is a never-ending education. The process of mixing ingredients is mingled with the knowledge of how to judge the actual feel of the dough to achieve the desired result. The bialy is a perfect example of a baked good that goes against common baking rules. Wet, sticky dough proofed for long periods may not appear correct, but it is the secret to bubbly crumbs and crispy crust. My bialy recipe brings back the memories of the special rolls dearly remembered from my days in Brooklyn as a young man.

Starter Dough

1 cup warm water, 80-100°F, in 4-cup bowl or measuring cup
1 teaspoon active or rapid-rise powder yeast
1½ cups all-purpose flour (bleached or unbleached)
1 teaspoon sugar

Onion Filling

3 tablespoons minced fried onion
2 teaspoons extra-virgin olive oil

Fresh Dough

1 cup warm water
2 teaspoons active or rapid-rise yeast
Starter dough (from the night before)
2½ cups all-purpose flour
1 tablespoon sugar
1½ tablespoons salt

Starter Dough

Activate the yeast in water according to the packet directions. Using a spoon, mix the flour and sugar into the water and yeast mixture until well-blended, loose, and sticky. Cover and let it rise (proof) for 8 to 10 hours to be used when making fresh dough later (preferably the next morning).

Onion Filling

Mix the ingredients in a small cup and let it sit until ready to fill the bialy wells.

Fresh Dough

Pour water into the mixing bowl of a stand mixer. Activate the yeast in water. Add the starter dough from the night before in the mixing bowl with a rubber spatula (it may look a little dry, but will moisten when placed in the stand mixer). Blend until the ingredients incorporate.

Add the remaining ingredients. Place the bowl on the stand mixer, and insert the mixing paddle (not the kneading hook). Allow the mixer to slowly blend the ingredients for 2 minutes until it is very loose (but not as loose as cake batter) and some of the dough sticks to the bottom of the bowl. It will be gooey, but will not pour like cake batter.

Coat an 18- x 12-inch baking pan with cooking oil (such as extra-virgin olive oil, canola oil, or vegetable oil).

Remove the dough from the mixing bowl onto a pan. You will notice that the gluten strands as most of the wet dough comes off the bowl. Break the round glob of wet dough into two halves and fold over into two (5-inch) round patties.

Cover with a towel and place in an oven warmed to 100°F (this should take 1 minute when the oven is set at 350°F). Turn off the oven and let the covered dough rise for 25 minutes.

After 25 minutes, remove from the oven. It should double in size.

Deflate the dough and form the patties again with a rubber spatula or wet hands. Repeat this process, again, for 25 minutes. Warm the oven to 100°F, but don't forget to turn it off while the dough is rising: you don't want it to bake yet.

Remove the pan, and place both patties on a floured surface. The dough will be very sticky, and needs to be rolled in the flour to cut manageably and form 6 to 8 bialys.

Lightly coat the pan with cornmeal and flour for the bottom of the bialys. Roll the dough into 4-ounce balls, and separate the dough into rows across the pan. Flatten the dough balls to 5-inch-diameter patties. Cover and place in the 100°F oven for 25 minutes.

Remove the pan, and set the oven to 425°F.

While the oven is heating, with a wet finger, form 1¼-inch well in the center of each patty, but do not deflate the patty outside of the well.

Evenly spoon the moist onion mixture into each well (about ½ teaspoon should suffice). Use all of the onion mixture.

Sprinkle a very light amount of onion powder, garlic, and flour on top of the bialys. Place in the heated oven for 16 to 19 minutes. Remove when lightly browned, but not dark. Let set until cooled (about 1 hour). If you prefer soft rather than crispy bialys, place them in a plastic bag.

Cinnamon Rolls

Serves 12

Cinnamon rolls were a highlight in my household growing up. They are great when bought from the bakery or supermarket, but homemade cinnamon rolls hot from the oven are the ultimate taste sensation. Here is a variation on my mother-in-law's recipe for her ring cake, which uses sweet roll dough. You can also use a 16 oz. package of frozen sweet roll dough.

Story by Monica

1 cup boiling water
¾ cup shortening
½ cup sugar plus1 teaspoon sugar
1 teaspoon salt
2 eggs
½ cup cold water
2 packages dry yeast
2 tablespoons sugar
½ cup warm water
6 cups all-purpose flour
1 cup raisins

Icing
2 tablespoons butter, melted
1 cup confectioners' sugar
1 tablespoon milk
½ teaspoon vanilla

Pour boiling water over the shortening, sugar, and salt in a large bowl. In another bowl, mix the eggs with cold water. Dissolve the yeast and 2 tablespoons of sugar in warm water; let set until it starts to rise. Add the egg mixture to the shortening. Add yeast, and mix well. Add 4 cups of flour, and beat well with a mixer until smooth. Remove and stir in the remaining flour to make a soft dough. Refrigerate for 4 hours or overnight. Roll half of the dough at a time. Roll out each half to a 9- x 12-inch rectangle. Spread with softened butter, add raisins, and sprinkle with sugar and cinnamon. Roll up and cut each into 12 slices. Let rise for 1 hour. Bake at 325°F for 20 minutes or until browned.

Icing

Mix the butter and sugar. Add in confectioners' sugar slowly: a little at a time. Once smooth, add in milk and vanilla. Mix until creamy smooth. Glaze the rolls with icing. Serve warm.

Baked French Toast

Pat Hogeboom *(Central Islip, NY)*
Serves 6-8

> This is really a kind of bread pudding, but comes out crisper
> and tastes more like French toast. It is delicious and great for
> brunch or a group lunch.

1 loaf white bread (see page 12), cubed (a good rustic bread is fine,
too)
1 (8 oz.) package cream cheese
10 large eggs
½ cup maple syrup
1 cup milk

Line the bottom of an 11- x 13-inch pan with half the bread cubes.
Layer the cream cheese cubes on top of the bread. Place the remaining bread cubes on top. Beat the eggs, maple syrup, and milk together in a large bowl, and pour over the bread and cheese. Refrigerate overnight. Bake at 350°F until light golden brown (about 45
minutes). Cut into individual servings and serve.

Basic White Bread

Serves 6-8

¾ cup warm water
1 package active dry yeast
1 teaspoon salt
1½ tablespoons sugar
1 tablespoon vegetable shortening
½ cup milk
3 cups all-purpose flour
Butter, to grease bowl and bread pan

Using a large bowl, dissolve the yeast in water. Once dissolved, add salt, sugar, shortening, and milk, and stir. Mix in the flour a little at a time (you may not need all of the flour). The dough is ready when it forms a ball. Turn the dough out onto a floured surface and knead, adding more flour, if necessary, until the dough is nice and soft, but not tacky and sticking to your fingers. Put the dough in a buttered bowl; turn the dough to grease completely. Cover with a tea towel, and let rise in a warm spot for 1 hour. Punch down the dough, and then turn out, again, onto your floured surface and knead. You are ready to bake. Preheat an oven at 375°F. Form the dough into a loaf, and set in an 8½- x 4½- x 2½-inch buttered loaf pan. Cover and let rise for about 30 minutes to 1 hour or until doubled in size. Score the dough by slashing across the top with a sharp knife. Bake for about 45 minutes or until golden brown. Turn out the bread and cool on a baking rack.

You can also make rolls using this recipe. Follow the mixing procedure above. Let rise until doubled, and shape into 12 rolls. Place on a greased baking pan. Allow to rise until doubled, again (about another hour). Beat one egg, and add 1 tablespoon of water. Brush tops with this mixture. Sprinkle with sesame or poppy seeds. Bake at 375°F for about 25 minutes or until golden brown. Cool on baking rack or serve warm in a bread basket at the table.

Applesauce Oatmeal Muffins

Serves 12

> Every fall, my kitchen is filled with crates of apples from apple-picking. All different kinds, sweet and tart, combine to make applesauce coupled with another popular breakfast food, oatmeal. I always remember my husband's Aunt Pat, a small and perky woman, passing on her "Mom-Knowledge" of making treats using oatmeal in her cookies to satisfy the sweet tooth and add nourishment at the same time—just one of her tricks to feed her five children healthy foods without them realizing it.
>
> *Story by Monica*

1½ cups flour
1 tablespoon baking powder
½ teaspoon baking soda
1 teaspoon cinnamon
¼ teaspoon ground cloves
1 cup quick oats
¾ cups dark brown sugar, packed
¼ cup raisins
¼ cup walnuts
1 large egg, beaten
½ cup extra-virgin olive oil (or any of your favorite vegetable oils)
¾ cups milk
1 cup freshly made applesauce

Preheat an oven to 400°F. Using a 12-cup muffin tin, apply autumn-themed paper liners. Combine the flour, baking powder, baking soda, cinnamon, and cloves in a large bowl. Stir in the oats, brown sugar, raisins, and nuts. In a medium bowl, combine the egg, oil, milk, and applesauce, and blend together by hand. Stir this mixture into the dry ingredient mixture until just moist. Fill the prepared muffin tins with batter and bake for 23 to 25 minutes or until the tops spring back when touched.

For a surprise Halloween breakfast, use 1 cup of canned or cooked (cubed, microwaved, and mashed) pumpkin and 1½ teaspoons of pumpkin pie spice (1 teaspoon of cinnamon, ¼ teaspoon of ground ginger, and ¼ teaspoon of ground cloves).

Use Halloween themed paper liners.

Blueberry Scones

Serves 6

After having had proper scones in England, I have been on a quest for the perfect scone ever since. This recipe is nice and not too heavy. You may also use fresh cranberries instead of the blueberries. Adding a little orange zest with the cranberries does just that: zest it up. Serve with clotted cream, close your eyes, and enjoy. You will think that you are at high tea at Westminster Abbey.

Story by Monica

2 cups all-purpose flour
1 tablespoon baking powder
2 tablespoons sugar
1 teaspoon salt
5 tablespoons butter, room temperature
1 cup blueberries, fresh or frozen and thawed
1¼ cups heavy cream, divided, plus extra to brush over tops

Lemon Glaze
2 cups powdered sugar
2 tablespoons butter
Lemon zest
1 cup water

Preheat an oven to 400°F. Lightly grease a medium-sized baking sheet. Sift the flour, baking powder, sugar, and salt into a large bowl. Add the butter in chunks. Add the blueberries and heavy cream. After lightly flouring your work surface, roll out your dough into a log and flatten to about 1¼-inch thick. Cut the log into triangles to make each scone. Using a pastry brush, brush the top of each scone with the rest of the heavy cream. Then place on the prepared baking sheet and bake for 10 to 15 minutes or until golden.

Lemon Glaze

Combine all the glaze ingredients in a saucepan on top of the stove and bring to a boil. Let the sauce simmer until thick. Drizzle on the scones right before serving.

Mock Clotted Cream

1 cup whipping cream
½ teaspoon vanilla
½ tablespoon sugar

Mix all the ingredients in a large bowl until you have passed the whipped cream phase and the cream appears overbeaten and too thick to use as a topping. Use immediately to spread upon your scones.

Making traditional English Devonshire clotted cream requires unpasteurized milk, which I have never seen in my New York grocery store. I prefer to use my updated American version, which I created when I accidentally overwhipped the cream to serve atop pudding about 20 years ago: whipping cream, a little sugar, and vanilla extract. You could also include mascarpone, which can be found in specialty cheese shops.

Blueberry Vegan Scones

Liz Finnegan *(Islip, NY)*
Makes 16

Liz has been a vegetarian for years now. Both her son and his girlfriend are vegans, and when Liz brought in these homemade vegan blueberry scones to share at work, I asked her to please ask for the recipe so I could share it. Even if you are not vegetarian, these delicious treats are a healthy alternative to traditional scone recipes. I find that having a mix of traditional and alternative recipes on hand allows me to be ready for any of my guests' food preferences without having to research special recipes at the last minute.

Story by Monica

2 cups all-purpose flour
1 cup whole-wheat flour
2 tablespoons baking powder
¼ cup sugar
¼ teaspoon salt
⅓ cup extra-virgin olive oil
½ cup soy cream
¾ cup rice milk
2 teaspoons apple cider vinegar
1½ cups fresh blueberries
1 teaspoon raw sugar

Preheat an oven to 400°F. Lightly grease a cookie sheet. Using a large mixing bowl, sift the flours, baking powder, ¼ cup of sugar, and salt. Add oil, soy cream, rice milk, and apple cider vinegar. Mix until combined so the dough is clumpy, but not sticky. Fold in the blueberries. Drop by ¼ cupfuls onto the greased cookie sheet and flatten the tops to rounds. Sprinkle with a bit of raw sugar. Bake 12 to 15 minutes or until firm. Serve warm.

You can omit the blueberries from this recipe to create different kinds of scones. For kid-friendly chocolate chip scones, add 1 teaspoon of vanilla extract to the liquid ingredients, and add 2 tablespoons of sugar, then folding in ½ cup of chocolate chips and ½ cup of raisins. To make a maple-nut version, just add 2 teaspoons of maple extract to your liquid ingredients plus 2 tablespoons of sugar, then folding in 1½ cups of chopped walnuts and/or pecans.

Banana Bread

Serves 8

1¾ cups sifted flour
¼ whole-wheat flour, sifted
2 teaspoons baking powder
½ teaspoon baking soda
½ teaspoon salt
¼ cup butter
¼ cup white sugar
¼ cup brown sugar
2 eggs, beaten
2 bananas, medium-ripe, mashed
¼ teaspoon banana extract
½ cup buttermilk
¼ cup walnuts, chopped

Sift the flours, baking powder, baking soda, and salt. Cream the butter
and sugars; add eggs, banana, banana extract, and buttermilk. Mix
with the flour mixture a little at a time. Mix in the walnuts. Pour into a
greased loaf pan and bake at 350°F for 1 hour or until a skewer placed
in the center comes out clean. Cool on a bakers' rack for 10 minutes.
Turn out of the pan and fully cool on the rack. Slice and serve.

Harvest Pumpkin Bread

Serves 8

1½ cups sifted all-purpose flour
¼ cup whole-wheat flour, sifted
¼ teaspoon double-acting baking powder
1 teaspoon baking soda
½ teaspoon salt
1 teaspoon cinnamon
½ teaspoon ground cloves
1 cup white sugar
⅓ cup light brown sugar, loosely packed
⅓ cup butter, melted
2 eggs
1 cup pumpkin, skinned, cubed, cooked, and mashed
⅓ cup milk
1 teaspoon vanilla
½ cup walnuts, chopped
½ cup raisins

Preheat an oven to 350°F. Sift together the flours, baking powder, baking soda, salt, cinnamon, and clove. Beat the sugars, butter, and eggs until fluffy. Mix in the pumpkin well. Add in the dry ingredients alternately with the milk and vanilla. Mix well. Fold in the nuts and raisins. Pour the batter into a greased loaf pan, and bake for 1 hour or until a skewer comes out clean. Cool on a bakers' rack for 10 minutes. Turn out of the pan and continue to cool on the rack. Slice and serve.

Easter Bread Ring

Yields 1 loaf

Many of my neighbors made this bread when I was growing up in East New York, Brooklyn. It was an Easter tradition, and many bakeries even decorated their front windows with larger versions of it. You can dye your eggs using an Easter egg coloring kit, which is plenty of fun for the kids. When my son was in the fourth grade, he made a project for the science fair using natural dyes made from colors extracted from various fruits, vegetables, and spices. That was the first year that we used his newly discovered method to dye our Easter eggs. When serving this bread at your brunch buffet, you'll want to double the recipe, as it is really popular with adults and children.

Story by Monica

Bread

5 colored Easter eggs
¼ cup white sugar
1 teaspoon salt
1 (25 oz.) package active dry yeast
3½ cups all-purpose flour, divided
⅔ cup milk
6 tablespoons butter
3 eggs
½ cup candied pineapple, orange, and mango, diced small
⅓ cup blanched almonds, chopped
½ teaspoon anise seed
1 egg
½ teaspoon water

Icing

1 tablespoon milk
1 cup confectioners' sugar
¼ teaspoon vanilla extract
2 drops orange oil
¼ orange zest

Bread

Parboil and color your Easter eggs and set aside.

In a large bowl, blend the white sugar, salt, and yeast with 2 cups of flour. Combine the ⅔ cup of milk with the butter, and heat slowly in a saucepan until warm and the butter is partially melted. Let cool for 5 minutes. Pour the milk into the dry ingredients and beat for 2 minutes on medium using an electric mixer. Add eggs, one at a time, beating well after each addition. Gradually add the remaining flour, ½ cup at a time, using the slowest speed until a thick batter is formed. Beat on medium speed for another 2 minutes. Stir in enough flour until a soft dough forms that leaves the sides of the bowl. Place the dough on a lightly floured flat surface and knead for 10 minutes (dough will be sticky: you may add a little flour just to be able to handle it, but don't let it get too dry, as it should remain slightly sticky). Place the dough in a greased bowl, being certain to cover all the sides. Cover with a slightly dampened tea towel for 1 hour or until doubled in size. While the dough is rising, combine the fruit, nuts, and anise seed. Once the dough has risen, return to a lightly floured surface and knead in the fruit mixture. Divide the dough into two equal portions, and roll each piece into a 24-inch long rope, tucking in the fruit and nuts, if necessary. Loosely twist the two ropes together to form a ring, and place on a greased cookie sheet, pinching the ends together and tucking them under. Brush with an egg wash of 1 egg hand-beaten with ½ teaspoon of water. Make an indent in the dough for each colored egg. Push the eggs deeply into the dough as far as possible. Cover the dough, again, loosely wrapping in plastic wrap this time and allowing it to rise for an hour (it will double in size, again). Once risen, bake in a preheated oven at 350°F for about 35 minutes or until a skewer is inserted and comes out clean. Cool on a bakers' rack. Once cooled, drizzle on the icing, being careful not to touch the eggs.

Icing

Mix together 1 tablespoon of whole milk and confectioners' sugar a little at a time until smooth. Add the vanilla, orange oil, and orange zest, and mix in well.

How to Naturally Dye Easter Eggs

Raspberries, blueberries, and turmeric show the best color when dying Easter eggs naturally. For each of the berries, place ½ cup of berries into a microwave-safe glass bowl covered with a white paper towel, and microwave for 1 minute to begin reducing them. Add ⅛ to ¼ cup of boiling water, and press down onto the berries with a small masher or the back of a spoon, making it into a liquid and extracting the color (the less water that is used, the deeper the color will be). Strain out seeds and/or skin for a smooth liquid, and dip the hardboiled (or parboiled) eggs, rotating in the liquid for full coverage. Set to dry on a plate, in the egg carton, or on a small shot glass. The raspberries have a lovely pinkish red color, and the blueberries are a purplish blue.

If using turmeric, which gives a yellowish orange color, use 3 tablespoons of turmeric with ⅛ to ¼ cup of boiling water, strain, and filter until you are left with a clear yellow liquid. Color the eggs as described above.

Crumb Cake

Gretel Carlin *(Stony Brook, NY)*

Serves 16

2 cups sifted cake flour
1 teaspoon baking powder
½ teaspoon baking soda
¼ teaspoon salt
½ cup butter
1 (8 oz.) package cream cheese
1¼ cups sugar
2 eggs
1 teaspoon vanilla
¼ cup milk

Crumbs
2½ cups cake flour
1 cup sugar
3 teaspoons cinnamon
1 cup melted butter
¼-½ confectioners' sugar, for sprinkling

Preheat an oven to 350°F. Grease and flour a 9- x 13-inch baking pan.

Sift together the cake flour, baking powder, baking soda, and salt. In a separate bowl, cream the butter and cream cheese until well-blended. Gradually beat in the sugar. Add eggs and vanilla. Add the flour mixture alternately with milk, and mix with a fork. Pour the batter into a prepared pan.

Crumbs

Combine the flour, sugar, and cinnamon. Stir in the melted butter, and mix with a fork. Squeeze the mixture together to make crumbs, and place on the batter. Bake for 35 to 40 minutes or until a wooden skewer comes out clean. Cool for 10 minutes on a rack, and sprinkle with confectioners' sugar.

Poppy Seed Babka

Serves 12

2 sticks unsalted butter
4 large eggs
1 cup sugar
⅞ cup potato starch
1 cup wheat flour
1½ tablespoons baking powder
⅓ cup milk
½ teaspoon almond extract
1 cup poppy seeds

Preheat an oven to 300°F. Grease and flour a loaf pan. Mix the softened butter until creamy. Add eggs, sugar, and potato starch. Sift together the flour and baking powder, and add to the previous mixture. Add milk, almond extract, and poppy seeds. Bake for 50 minutes. Let sit in a pan for 10 minutes, and then invert and cool on a wire rack.

If you find that your dough is too sticky, add a little flour. Add a little more milk if you find that your dough is too dry. You will feel when it is the right consistency.

Savory Brunch Ring

Serves 4–6

4 slices bacon
⅓ cup plus 1 tablespoon milk
4 eggs, slightly beaten
¼ cup chopped red pepper
2 tablespoons butter
1 (8 oz.) can refrigerated crescent dinner rolls
½ cup shredded cheddar cheese
½ cup shredded Monterey Jack cheese
¼ cup fresh cilantro, chopped
½ cup sour cream
1 cup salsa
Salt and pepper, to taste

Preheat an oven to 375°F. Line a large cookie sheet with parchment paper. Cook the bacon, turning once, and remove from the heat just before it gets crispy. Drain on a paper towel, chop, and set aside. In a medium bowl, beat ⅓ cup of milk and the eggs. Stir in the pepper and cook in 2 tablespoons of butter on top of the stove in a clean skillet for 5 to 6 minutes or until thickened, but not fully cooked (do not overcook).

Separate your dough into eight triangles. On your lined cookie sheet, arrange the triangles in a circle overlapping each other. Leave a hole in the middle point of the triangle pointing toward the center, making a big circle in the middle (like you would a coffee cake). Sprinkle on the bacon, one-third of the cheese, the eggs, salt and pepper to taste, and another one-third of the cheese. Pull back the point of the triangle up over the mixture, tucking in at the far edge. Brush with 1 tablespoon of milk and sprinkle on the remaining cheese. Bake for 20 to 25 minutes or until lightly browned. Place on a serving plate and sprinkle with cilantro. Slice and serve with sour cream and salsa on the side.

Peanut Butter and Jam Muffins

Amy Acierno, Miss Amy's Jams and Preserves *(Patchogue, NY)*
Serves 12

2 cups flour
3 tablespoons sugar
1 teaspoon baking powder
¾ cup peanut butter
1 egg
1½ cups milk
⅓ cup strawberry jam

Preheat an oven to 350°F. Grease nonstick muffin cups or use foil baking cups. Mix the flour, sugar, and baking powder in a large bowl. Beat the peanut butter and egg in another bowl with a wooden spoon until smooth. Add milk a little at a time, stirring after each addition. Pour the peanut butter mixture over the dry ingredients and fold in until just moistened (mixture will be stiff like a dough). Spoon 2 scant tablespoons of batter into each muffin cup. Top with 1 teaspoon of jam, and then cover with 1 tablespoon of batter. Bake for 20 to 25 minutes or until the tops spring back when touched.

Strawberry Jam

Yields 6 (8-ounce) jars

4 cups strawberries, hulled, rinsed, and mashed
8 cups sugar
2 packs pectin
2 cups water

Mix the strawberries and sugar, and let stand. Mix 2 packages of pectin with 2 cups of water. Boil for 1 minute. Turn off, and add the berries and sugar. Let set for 2 minutes and stir. Pour into freezer containers and freeze.

Three Herb Breakfast Bake

Serves 6

> My friend Ann Inoue is a wonderful cook, and belongs to a
> community farm on Long Island, New York, where her family
> volunteers to plant and weed. In turn, they reap the harvested
> fresh fruits and vegetables throughout the summer and fall.
> She brought me a bunch of leeks last year, and I prepared this
> Middle Eastern-influenced dish using turmeric, which is much
> touted for its healthful attributes, along with fresh herbs from
> my garden.
>
> *Story by Monica*

½ cup chopped cilantro plus 2 tablespoons for garnish
½ cup chopped dill
½ cup chopped parsley
½ teaspoon ground turmeric
12 eggs, lightly beaten
1 large Russet potato, peeled, grated, and blanched
1 large leek, quartered lengthwise, thinly sliced
Kosher salt and freshly ground black pepper, to taste

Stir together the cilantro, dill, parsley, turmeric, eggs, potato, leek,
salt, and pepper in a large bowl. Pour the egg mixture into a large
lightly greased casserole dish, and bake at 350°F for about 30 minutes
or until completely set. Garnish with cilantro.

Caviar Éclair

Serves 6

Pâte á Choux

1¼ cups water
1½ sticks (¾ cup) unsalted butter, cut into pieces
½ teaspoon salt
1½ cups unbleached flour
4-6 large eggs

Éclairs

1 recipe pâte á choux
1 beaten egg
5 slices smoked salmon
8 ounces whipped cream cheese
½ cup dairy sour cream
4 ounces black caviar
Finely chopped fresh dill, to taste
Freshly ground black pepper, to taste

Pâte á Choux

In a heavy saucepan, bring water to a boil with butter and salt over high heat. Reduce the heat to medium. Add flour all at once and beat with a wooden spoon until the mixture pulls away from the sides of the pan, forming a dough.

Transfer the dough to the bowl of a standing electric mixer and beat in four eggs, one at a time, on high speed, beating well after each addition. The batter should be stiff enough to just hold soft peaks and fall softly from a spoon. If the batter is too stiff, in a small bowl, beat the remaining two eggs lightly, one at a time, and add to the batter a little at a time, beating on high speed until the batter is the desired consistency.

Éclairs

Fill a pastry bag fitted with a small plain tip with warm pâte á choux.

Butter a baking sheet. Pipe out 2-inch lengths of the pâte á choux (they should look like stripes of yellow toothpaste). Top with a second strip of pastry dough. Form 20 such miniature éclairs.

Brush the tops of the éclairs with the beaten egg. Bake according to the pâte á choux directions, and cool completely.

Cut each piece of salmon into quarters and reserve. Slice the éclairss horizontally into halves. Spread a thin layer of cream cheese in the bottom of each éclair and lay a piece of salmon on top. Spread a thin layer of sour cream on the salmon and top with a dab of caviar. Sprinkle with dill and freshly ground black pepper. Return the tops to the éclairs.

Just-Picked Apple Bread Pudding

Serves 4

1 cup homemade white bread (see page 12), toasted and cubed
1 cup McIntosh apples, peeled and cubed
2½ cups Red Delicious apples, peeled and cubed
¼ cup raisins
½ cup sugar
½ cup light brown sugar
1½ teaspoons cinnamon
¼ cup butter, melted

Preheat an oven to 350°F. Grease a 1½-quart baking casserole dish. Line the casserole dish with the bread, and layer on the apples and raisins. Combine the sugar and cinnamon, and sprinkle over the apples. Drizzle with melted butter. Cover and bake for 50 to 60 minutes. Serve warm with whipped cream (see page 120).

> For a late summer variation, you can also substitute the apples with freshly picked peaches. Wash, skin, pit, and slice the peaches, then soaking them in ¼ cup of brandy for an hour before adding to the recipe for a more pungent flavor.

Grandma LaCapria's Biscotti

Loren Christie *(Patchogue, NY)*
Serves 24
Makes 3 dozen

> Not many people are fortunate to know their great-grandparents. I consider the close relationship I had with my Italian great-grandmother as a blessing that influenced the person who I am today, because her unconditional adoration gave me confidence. Smelling Grandma's cookies is like having her standing beside me. They remind me of how loved that I felt around her. Making one of her recipes is like giving myself—and whomever I bake for—the gift of her presence. Her biscotti contains almonds, but you can add whatever you want.

5 cups flour
2 cups sugar
1 tablespoon baking powder
5 eggs
2 sticks butter
Almonds, dried fruit, and/or other nuts (optional)

Preheat an oven to 350°F. Mix the sugar, baking powder, and flour in a bowl. Dump the mixture onto a large cookie sheet and make a hole in the middle. Fill the hole with eggs and butter, and then combine everything until it looks like dough. Divide the dough into two loaves. Place the loaves on greased pans, and bake for 25 minutes or until lightly brown. Remove from the oven and cut the loaves crosswise into ½-inch slices. Lay the slices cut-side down on the same pan, making sure that the pieces do not touch. Return to the oven and bake for 5 minutes. Store the cookies in a tightly covered container.

Part II

LUNCH

Part II

LUNCH

Individual Turkey Tarts

LUNCH

Rainy days stuck in the house can sometimes be a challenge when you're faced with the task of thinking up fun activities. There are many hours in a day, so your creative juices are called upon. Board games, movies, and charades all go a long way, but they work up quite an appetite.

When it comes time for lunch, simply check out what is in the refrigerator or pantry. Chances are you'll already have on hand common baking ingredients like flour and eggs. Whip up Savory Corn Muffins (page 48) or Individual Turkey Tarts (page 36). You're also likely to find dried herbs and tomato sauce tucked away in the pantry for times like these. Why not make pizza? You can prepare your own dough (see page 68) or try making French Bread Pizza (page 55). Making pizza is a fun group activity that will keep everyone occupied, and the end result is a delicious homemade meal. Each person can choose their own toppings, and everyone will have fun arranging the meats and vegetables on their own slices. Clean up is pretty easy, too, since there are usually no leftovers to worry about storing, and baking pizza doesn't require many pots and pans.

While you have the oven warmed, why not also make a snack for your next at-home movie night? Try making your own Zucchini Pumpkin Muffins (page 43) using the pumpkins and zucchini in your vegetable storage bins. Freshly baked Gingerbread (page 53) can always find a spot on the agenda, as can Cheddar Cheese Bread (page 54) with Olive Tapenade (page 45) and Sun-Dried Tomato Tapenade (page 46)—tasty choices using just a few of your refrigerator and pantry staples.

Before you know it, the rainy day has passed, as you have played games and shared a nice lunch together. Passing on traditions happens naturally when you cook together. Getting creative in the kitchen and using what you have stored in your pantry or refrigerator can turn an otherwise dreary afternoon into something extra special and memorable.

Individual Turkey Tarts

Serves 8

> Finding challenging ways to use leftover turkey from a big holiday meal is half the fun; the other half is eating it. Little individual savory tarts can turn lunch into something special when these mini-pot pies are served.

Two Crust Pastry

4 cups flour

2 teaspoons salt

1 cup shortening

½ cup butter

¼ cup ice water (or as needed)

Filling

½ cup onion, diced

½ cup celery, diced

½ cup carrots, diced

4 tablespoons butter

½ cup frozen peas

3 tablespoons fresh parsley, finely chopped

½ cup all-purpose flour

1 teaspoon salt

½ teaspoon freshly ground mixed peppercorns

2½ cups milk

4 cups cooked white meat turkey breast, shredded

1 cup dry white wine

1 cup Parmesan cheese, grated

Two Crust Pastry

Preheat an oven to 475°F.

Make sure that all the materials are ice-cold. Sift the flour and salt. Blend the shortening and butter into the flour. Add just enough ice water a little at a time to hold the dough together. Chill for an hour, and then divide into 8 parts and roll ¼-inch thick. Roll each into a circle, and fit over the back of a medium muffin cup or 6-ounce ramekin to create 8 pastry shells. Make pleats so the pastry will fit closely. Prick with a fork and bake on a cookie sheet for 5 to 8 minutes or until golden brown. Cool completely. Remove from the pans.

Filling

Reduce the oven temperature to 400°F.

Sauté the onion, celery, and carrots in butter until al dente. Add the frozen peas and parsley, and cook for 2 more minutes. Stir in the flour, salt, and pepper. Remove from the heat, and then gradually stir in the milk. Heat to boiling over medium heat, stirring constantly. Bring to a boil for 1 minute, continuing to stir constantly. Add in turkey and wine; heat for 3 more minutes. Fill the pastry shells, sprinkle with Parmesan cheese, and bake for 15 to 20 minutes or until the cheese begins to brown.

Rustic Three Cheese Tart

Serves 8

> I recently sampled this at a cheese tasting, and just had to make it myself. The smoky flavor of the gouda is memorable. It is easy to make using phyllo dough, which can be bought in the freezer section of most supermarkets, much to my delight.

6 sheets phyllo dough
2 ounces butter, melted
¼ cup sharp white cheddar cheese, shredded
½ cup smoked gouda cheese, shredded
½ cup gruyere cheese, shredded
3 eggs, beaten lightly
½ cup milk
¼ cup cream
1 tablespoon chives, finely chopped
2 tablespoons parsley, finely chopped

Preheat the oven to 350°F. If frozen, defrost the phyllo dough and use 6 sheets. Cover with damp paper towels to keep moist while working with them. Place the first layer on a surface and brush with butter, continuing the same procedure with all the phyllo sheets. Grease a 9-inch baking tin with butter. Line the tin with your prepared phyllo. Combine all of the remaining ingredients, and pour into a pan. Bake for 35 to 40 minutes or until lightly browned, and set in the middle. You may test for doneness with a skewer that comes out clean when done. Serve with an assortment of Greek olives and marinated grape tomatoes (see next page).

Marinated Grape Tomatoes

Serves 8

1 cup grape tomatoes, sliced in half
¼ cup extra-virgin olive oil
1 tablespoon oregano
1 garlic clove, minced
⅛ cup balsamic vinegar
¹⁄₁₆ teaspoon sea salt
¹⁄₁₆ teaspoon black pepper, freshly ground

Mix all the ingredients and refrigerate for at least 1 hour.

Veggie Pot Pies

Serves 6

Cutting down on meat throughout the week and replacing several meals with a vegetable alternative is a good habit to get into. Adding more vegetables into your diet makes for a healthier lifestyle. You can experiment with different vegetables using this same basic recipe.

1 Idaho potato, washed, peeled, and cubed
4½ ounces pumpkin, peeled and cubed
1 large carrot, scraped and sliced to ½ inch
4½ ounces cauliflower
2 tablespoons water
1 medium onion, finely chopped
1 red bell pepper, diced
1 tablespoon extra-virgin olive oil

Sauce
1⅔ ounces salted butter
2 tablespoons whole-wheat flour
1½ cups light cream
1 cup cheddar cheese, shredded
2 egg yolks
¼ teaspoon sea salt (or to taste)
¼ teaspoon cayenne pepper
¼ teaspoon parsley, dried
2 sheets puff pastry (see page 192)
1 egg, beaten
3 teaspoons sesame seeds

Preheat an oven to 425°F. Grease 6 individual ramekins (1 cup each). Place the potato, pumpkin, carrot, cauliflower, and water in a microwave-safe dish, and cover with a paper towel. Cook on high for 20 minutes or until the potato is fork-split.

Remove, pouring off any remaining water. Set aside. Sauté the onion and red pepper in oil for 2 to 3 minutes. Mix into the vegetables.

Sauce

Melt the butter and add in flour. Stir over low heat for 2 minutes. Add cream gradually, stirring until completely smooth. Continue stirring for 3 minutes until boiled and thickened. Remove from the heat and cool slightly, then adding the cheese and egg yolks, and stirring until completely combined. Season with salt, cayenne pepper, and parsley. Mix the vegetables and sauce together. Fill each ramekin. Cut 6 circles from the pastry (see page 192) and fit on top of the pot pies, pressing the edges around to seal. Brush with the beaten egg and sprinkle with sesame seeds. Bake for 30 minutes or until golden brown.

Swiss Tarts

Mary Carlin *(East Meadow, NY)*
Serves 8

2 pastry crusts (see page 191)
2 eggs
½ cup Swiss cheese, grated
1 teaspoon flour
¼ teaspoon nutmeg
¼ teaspoon salt

Chill the pastry while making the filling. Beat the eggs thoroughly
and stir in the remaining ingredients. Preheat an oven to 425°F.
Roll the pastry very thin on a lightly floured surface. Cut circles of
the pastry large enough to cover the bottom and sides of 16 to 18
very small tart pans, allowing a little excess dough for a rim. Fill
about halfway with the cheese filling and pinch the pastry rim together with your fingers (they should look like rosettes). Bake for
10 minutes. Serve hot (if you have any leftover pastry, try filling
it with bits of vegetables and cheese or sautéed onions and mushrooms, and bake until golden brown, about 10 minutes).

These can also be frozen before baking. Bake for 10 minutes if
thawed or 20 minutes if frozen.

Zucchini Pumpkin Muffins

Yields 12

2 cups flour
1/16 teaspoon sea salt
1 teaspoon cinnamon
1/4 teaspoon nutmeg
2 zucchinis, washed, skin on, grated
3/4 cup pumpkin, cubed and cooked
1/2 cup pistachios, shelled and chopped
2 eggs
1 cup milk
3 ounces butter, melted

Preheat an oven to 415°F. Grease a 12-cup muffin tin with butter.
Sift the flour, salt, cinnamon, and nutmeg into a bowl. Add the zucchini, pumpkin, and pistachios. Combine the eggs, milk, and butter
in a separate bowl, and whisk vigorously. Combine the egg mixture
with the flour mixture. Do not over-mix. Divide the batter into the 12
muffin cups, and bake for 15 to 25 minutes or until a skewer comes
out clean. Leave in the tin for 2 minutes, and then turn out onto a
wire rack to cool.

No-Knead Ciabatta Bread

Harry Myers *(Lipan, TX)*
Serves 8

No matter what I did, my breads always came out a little dense. What was the secret to making an airy, bubbly inside with a crisp crust, like the ciabatta at the bakery? It took years to discover the secret. Now, the answer to making the much-loved ciabatta loaf is so simple that an inexperienced baker will succeed the first time. Homemade artisan bread will please everyone you serve it to: even with just a few pats of butter, it will disappear before your eyes.

This is a must-try recipe. No electric mixing is needed. If you start this recipe around 1 p.m., it will be baked and ready to eat the next morning around 9 a.m. The key is the long proofing (rise) and tasty fermentation. During baking, you may smell vinegar. Don't worry, it is just the fermentation baking out. The bread will taste delicious.

4 cups all-purpose flour plus extra for sprinkling
½ teaspoon powdered yeast
1½ teaspoons salt
2 cups warm water
Dash olive oil
Dash cornmeal

In a mixing bowl, add the first four ingredients. Stir until wet and sticky after a couple of minutes. Cover with plastic wrap for 18 hours.
Uncover after 18 hours, and you will find a bubbly and gooey dough. Punch down.
On a 12- x 18-inch baking pan, spread a light coating of olive oil, and sprinkle with cornmeal and flour.
Place the dough on a pan and fold over with a rubber spatula. With wet hands, spread the dough to 12 inches long and 5 inches wide, and shape into a flat loaf.

Spread a light amount of flour over the top and cover with towel. On a countertop, let it rest for 2 hours. The dough will spread more than it will rise. It will bake and rise to about 2 inches in the middle—the way that ciabatta should be in order to slice it so the top and bottom are a little flat.

Set an oven at 425°F, and place the dough on the center rack for 35 minutes or until light golden brown.

Olive Tapenade

Serves 8

Making tapenades is easy and quick, and they are perfect for any quick lunch or appetizer at a cocktail party served with homemade bread. This recipe pairs nicely with Ciabatta Bread (see previous page).

1 clove garlic, diced
1¾ cups mixed purple and black Greek olives, pitted and chopped
2 tablespoons anchovy paste
2 tablespoons capers
1 teaspoon fresh rosemary, chopped fine
1 teaspoon fresh thyme, chopped fine
4 tablespoons lemon juice
4 tablespoons extra-virgin olive oil
Sea salt and white pepper to taste

In a blender, mix until all the ingredients are combined. Do not let it turn into a paste: the mixture should be coarse.

Sun-Dried Tomato Tapenade

Serves 8

1 cup sun-dried tomatoes (or home-dried)
½ cup kalamata olives, pitted
2 tablespoons basil
⅛ teaspoon oregano
¼ teaspoon sea salt
¼ teaspoon freshly ground mixed peppercorns
2 tablespoons lemon juice
1 clove garlic, finely minced
2 teaspoons extra-virgin olive oil

Roughly mix all the ingredients (except the oil). Transfer to a bowl and mix in olive oil. Serve on toasted French bread (see page 77) or crackers.

If unable to find sun-dried tomatoes in the store, you can dry them at home in your oven. You will need 1 pound of plum tomatoes and salt to cover. Cut the tomatoes in half and place on a cookie sheet, cut-side up. Sprinkle with salt and bake at 250°F for 8 to 10 hours. Tomatoes will look darker and wrinkled when they are done. Pack in olive oil with 1 tablespoon of parsley and 2 cloves of garlic. Use in recipes; can be stored in the refrigerator.

Party-Size Mexican Grilled Cheese

Serves 4-6

1 cup Monterey Jack cheese, shredded
1 cup cheddar cheese, shredded
8 slices homemade white bread (see page 12)
4 teaspoons salted butter
3 eggs
1¼ cups milk
½ teaspoon chili powder
2 pickled jalapeño peppers, diced
¼ teaspoon salt
½ teaspoon smoky barbecue sauce
2 beefsteak tomatoes, sliced
¼ cup fresh cilantro, finely chopped

Grease the bottom of an 8-inch square casserole. Toss the two cheeses and set aside. Place four slices of bread in the bottom of the dish and cover with half of the cheese mixture. Butter the next four slices of bread and place on top of the cheese layer. Spread the remainder of the cheese on the bread slices. Mix the eggs, milk, chili powder, jalapeños, and salt, beating until fluffy. Pour the mixture over the prepared bread and bake in a 350°F oven for 30 to 40 minutes.

Savory Corn Muffins

Serves 12

> I often make a basic muffin, and then go wild by either adding different flavors or topping them off with something that you wouldn't expect, like the chili in this recipe.

1½ cups flour
¾ cup cornmeal
4 tablespoons sugar
3 teaspoons baking powder
1 teaspoon salt
1 cup milk
1 egg, beaten
3 tablespoons butter, melted
1 cup cooked corn, cut off the cob
2 cups chili without beans

Preheat an oven to 400°F. Sift the dry ingredients. Add milk, egg, butter, and corn. Mix well and fill greased muffin cups halfway. Add a tablespoon of chili and 2 tablespoons or batter to the top or each muffin. Bake for 30 to 40 minutes.

Challah Bread

Serves 8-10

New York City is the city that never sleeps, and when you are hungry for a late-night snack, you can find just about any type of restaurant open for business. Kiev was a famous Ukrainian restaurant on the Lower East Side, a haven for my friends and me after a night of dancing and listening to the music of Patti Smith or The Talking Heads in their heyday. You could find colorful people of all ages and nationalities dining at Kiev. The biggest treat for me was their thick slices of warm, homemade challah bread slathered with butter—perfect for dipping into hot chicken soup. They closed their doors for good several years ago, but my love for challah lives on.

Story by Monica

Sponge
1⅓ cups lukewarm water
¼ cup sugar
1 tablespoon active dry yeast

Dough
3½ cups bread flour
1 large egg
¼ cup vegetable oil
1 teaspoon salt
1 egg white, beaten

Sponge

Pour the water into a large bowl. Dissolve the sugar in the water, and add the yeast. Let stand for about 10 minutes. It should be bubbly.

Dough

Mix in 1 cup of flour and combine to form a slurry. Add the egg, oil, and salt. Add more flour in stages until too difficult to stir. Knead by hand until you have a slightly sticky ball of dough. Turn the dough out onto a floured surface and knead for 5 to 10 minutes until the dough is smooth and elastic. Place into an oiled bowl and cover with a damp cloth for 1½ hours or until doubled in volume. Knead the dough a second time, and then shape into loaves. Divide in two, and then divide each half again, into three and braid, forming two braided rolls. Place the loaves on a greased cookie sheet or baking stone, and cover with a linen dish towel for 45 minutes or until doubled, again. About 15 minutes before the end of the second rise, preheat the oven to 350°F. Brush the top with egg wash, and bake for 20 to 25 minutes or until they sound hollow when tapped.

Sponge is a small amount of yeast dough that is allowed to rise before being kneaded with the rest of the batch. Brushing with egg wash will add a light sheen to your bread.

Whole-Wheat Raisin Bread

Makes 1 loaf

1 cup warm water
1 package active dry yeast
½ cup raisins
3 tablespoons brown sugar
1 teaspoon salt
1 teaspoon cinnamon
2 tablespoons butter, sliced
2 cups all-purpose flour
1 cup whole-wheat flour
1 tablespoon oil, for brushing surface (optional)

Preheat an oven to 375°F. Dissolve the yeast in water, combine with the raisins, brown sugar, salt, cinnamon, and butter, and mix. In a large bowl, mix the flours, and then add to the yeast mixture. Mix until the dough forms a ball. Continue kneading for another minute. With lightly floured hands, remove the dough from the bowl. Place the dough in a greased bowl. Turn to coat completely. Cover. Let rise until doubled (about 1 hour). Shape into a loaf and place in a greased 8½- x 4½-inch loaf pan. Brush the top with oil. Let rise until doubled, again (about 1 hour). Bake for 30 to 40 minutes or until the loaf sounds hollow when tapped. Serve with fresh homemade Strawberry Jam (see page 27) or Vegetable Cream Cheese (see page 54).

Rye Bread

Makes 1 loaf

1 cup warm water
1 package active dry yeast
4 teaspoons molasses
1 teaspoon salt
2 tablespoons butter, sliced
2 cups all-purpose flour
1 cup rye flour
1 tablespoon caraway seeds

Preheat an oven to 375°F. Dissolve the yeast into water, and mix with molasses, salt, and butter. Blend. In a separate bowl, mix the flours and caraway seeds. Add to the yeast mixture and knead until a ball forms. When a ball forms, continue to knead for another minute. If the dough is too wet, add a little more flour. Knead again for 1 minute. With lightly floured hands, remove the dough from the bowl, and place in a greased bowl, turning to coat all the sides. Cover and let rise until doubled (about 1 hour). Shape into a loaf. Place in a greased 8½- x 4½- x 2½-inch loaf pan, and brush the top with oil. Let rise until doubled (about another hour). Bake for 30 to 40 minutes or until the loaf sounds hollow when tapped. Slice for sandwiches.

Gingerbread

Serves 10

1½ cups all-purpose flour
¼ teaspoon baking soda
1 teaspoon baking powder
¼ cup sugar
¼ teaspoon salt
1 teaspoon ground ginger
1 teaspoon cinnamon
¼ teaspoon ground cloves
½ cup milk
1 egg, beaten
½ cup light molasses
¼ cup oil

Preheat an oven to 350°F. Sift together the dry ingredients. Add milk to the beaten egg. Pour into the dry ingredients and stir until smooth. Stir in the molasses and oil. Pour the batter into a greased 8-inch square pan. Bake for 30 to 40 minutes. Cool on a wire rack for 10 minutes, and then turn out and either serve warm with fresh whipped cream (see page 120) or cool completely and store.

This gingerbread also makes a great Christmas gift for friends or family. After cooled completely, transfer to a flat surface, put a snowflake stencil on top of the cake, and sprinkle on confectioners' sugar to form a design. Place the finished bread in a holiday tin lined with a doily or waxed paper.

Cheddar Cheese Bread

Linda Eggebrecht *(Edwardville, KS)*
Serves 12

½ cup milk
1 egg, beaten
1½ cups biscuit mix
2 tablespoons parsley, chopped fine
1 teaspoon minced onion
1 cup cheddar cheese, shredded
¼ cup melted butter
1 egg, beaten

Preheat an oven to 350°F. Combine the milk and egg. Add biscuit mix, parsley, onion, and ½ cup of cheese. Pour into a greased 9-inch round pan. Sprinkle with the remaining cheese and pour on the butter. Bake for 25 minutes. Serve with Vegetable Cream Cheese.

Vegetable Cream Cheese

Serves 12

1 (8 oz.) package cream cheese
¾ cup red, yellow, and orange peppers, seeds removed, diced fine
⅛ cup green onion, diced fine
⅛ cup celery, strings removed, diced fine
1 teaspoon dried parsley

Mix together until completely blended. Refrigerate until ready to use. Serve on Cheddar Cheese Bread.

French Bread Pizza

Serves 6

> This is a great recipe to make a quick lunch in a pinch. Use French Bread to make a traditional pizza alternative. This is the most popular one with younger children. You can create a basic pizza using sauce and cheese, or try adding your favorite toppings and cheeses.

1 loaf French bread (see page 77), cut into 6 pieces
3 cups Italian marinara sauce
½ teaspoon dried oregano
½ teaspoon dried parsley
¾ cup fresh basil, finely chopped
¾ cup Parmesan cheese
1 cup fresh mozzarella, shredded

Preheat an oven to 350°F. Cut the French bread in half lengthwise, and then in thirds (you should have six slices on which to place your toppings). First, spread on ½ cup of sauce for each slice, and then sprinkle on the rest of the ingredients in the order listed, distributing equally between each slice. Transfer the French bread pizzas to a rectangular baking stone, and bake until the mozzarella is completely melted, being careful not to let it brown (about 15 to 20 minutes). Serve immediately with a salad.

Part III

APPETIZERS

Appetizers

When having an impromptu cocktail party, try serving savory appetizers like Quiche Lorraine (page 62) and finger foods like Leafy Pizza Swirls (page 68), accompanied by several sweets such as Fresh Pecan Cheesecake (page 63), in case some of your guests have already eaten dinner. For those who haven't eaten dinner, the savories are heartily welcomed, while for those friends who have managed to eat before they came, the sweets will really hit the spot.

Choose recipes that are seasonal and can appeal to both adults and children, especially around the Christmas and New Year's holidays, when families often drop by with their kids. Homemade Potato Chips (page 71) with your special French Onion Dip (page 72) and Mini-Quiches (page 66) will probably be the first to go on such occasions. The extra time that you have spent to make them lends to the warm feeling your guests will savor when visiting your home.

An added bonus is that many of these appetizers can be made ahead of time and popped into the oven as more guests arrive. You may have a steady stream of people who will pick at the buffet table while chatting and getting reacquainted, so it can be really helpful to have simple, yet delicious appetizers like Baked Brie (page 61) on hand.

Halloween is another time of year when you can't accurately pinpoint when your guests will arrive, because each age group of kids will trick-or-treat at their own rate. Then their parents will begin their quest for treats like Tangy Cheddar Cheese with Port Wine and Creamy Shrimp Dip (page 78) on toasted French Bread (page 77) after the kids are in the living room, happily rifling through *their* bags full of candy. It's now that the adults have a chance to mingle with each other after a long week of costume-making and pumpkin-carving.

Serving homemade appetizers (whether sweet or savory) will go a long way in extending goodwill and sharing the feeling of togetherness among friends and neighbors. Whenever you take the time to bake something from scratch, your guests will surely know how much extra effort you put into it, making them feel even more special in your life.

Baked Brie in Puff Pastry

Serves 8-12

> This is one of my favorite dishes at any gathering. It is so simple to make, yet so warm and full of flavor. This can even be made ahead and warmed in the oven just before you are ready to serve it. You can buy puff pastry in the freezer section of your supermarket or, of course, make your own (see page 192).
>
> *Story by Monica*

1 large sheet puff pastry (see page 192)
1 round brie cheese, rind left on
¾ cup apricot or raspberry jam
1 egg white, for brushing

Preheat an oven to 350°F. Place the puff pastry on a baking stone, and place the brie in the center of the pastry. Spread on the jam. Completely cover the top of the brie and jam with the pastry, and brush with egg white. Bake for 25 to 30 minutes or until golden brown. Let sit for 5 to 10 minutes before cutting and serving.

Try using ¾ cups of meatless mincemeat (see page 122) on top. Follow directions above, but instead of brushing with egg white, drizzle ¼ cup of Vermont maple syrup and 1 tablespoon of light brown sugar sprinkled on top. Bake and serve as above.

Quiche Lorraine

Mary Carlin (*East Meadow, NY*)
Serves 6

½ pound bacon
1 (9 in.) pastry crust (see page 191)
¼ pound Swiss or American cheese, grated
3 eggs
2 cups milk or light cream
1 teaspoon salt
¹⁄₁₆ teaspoon pepper
¹⁄₁₆ teaspoon cayenne pepper

Preheat an oven to 400°F. Fry the bacon until crisp. Crumble into the pastry-lined pie plate. Arrange the grated cheese over the bacon. Beat the eggs slightly with a whisk. Add milk (or cream) with seasonings. Blend and pour over the bacon and cheese in the pie plate. Bake for 35 to 45 minutes. Do not over-bake. Remove from the oven while the center still appears soft. Cool for 5 to 10 minutes before serving.

Fresh Pecan Cheesecake

Nora Rooney *(Raleigh, NC)*
Serves 12

> This is a fantastic cheesecake recipe from a friend's grandmother. My friends and I exchange recipes fairly regularly, and whenever a recipe is exceptionally good, it makes it to my personal collection of recipes. This cheesecake is one of those recipes. Fresh pecans are plentiful in the South, and their availability during the harvest season makes this recipe even more special.

Crust
¾ cup ground pecans
¾ cup graham cracker crumbs
3 tablespoons melted butter

Cheesecake
3 (8 oz.) packages cream cheese, room temperature
3 eggs, room temperature
1⅛ cups sugar
1½ teaspoons vanilla
1½ teaspoons almond extract
1 teaspoon lemon juice

Topping
1 pint sour cream
2 tablespoons sugar
1 teaspoon vanilla

Crust

Press the mixture into a 9-inch springform pan. Bake at 325°F for 10 minutes.

Cheesecake

Blend all the ingredients on medium speed for 10 minutes. Pour into a 9-inch springform pan, crust, and bake at 325°F for 40 to 50 minutes. Cool for 15 minutes before topping.

Topping

Preheat an oven to 450°F. Beat all the ingredients for 5 to 7 minutes and spread over the cake. Bake for 7 minutes. Chill overnight.

Gooey Popcorn Balls

Serves 10

10 cups popped corn
½ cup peanuts, shelled
½ cup pecan halves
1 cup dark brown sugar, packed firmly
½ cup butter
¼ cup maple syrup
¼ cup corn syrup
1½ teaspoons vanilla extract
½ teaspoon baking soda

Preheat an oven to 250°F. Combine the popcorn and nuts in a large roasting pan. Using a medium saucepan, combine the sugar, butter, maple syrup, and corn syrup. Bring to a boil for 2 minutes. Remove from the stove, and stir in the vanilla and baking soda. Pour over the popcorn mixture to coat. Bake for about 45 minutes, stirring twice. Remove, cool slightly, turn out onto waxed paper, and immediately shape into popcorn balls.

Mélange of Mini-Quiches

Yields 30

When you are having a get-together or throwing an extra special holiday party for the kids at home, try making several different kinds of mini-quiches as appetizers. Half the fun is biting into one and finding out which filling you have. Everyone will want to have one of each.

Story by Monica

Pastry Shells

1 cup all-purpose flour
1 stick butter (4 ounces), sliced
1/16 teaspoon salt (add 2 tablespoons sugar for fruit tarts)
3 tablespoons water

Filling

2 eggs
2/3 cup milk
1 pinch nutmeg (optional)
Selected fillings (see note)

Pastry Shells

Preheat an oven to 400°F. Put the flour, butter, and salt in a large mixing bowl. Rub together with your fingertips to reach the consistency of bread crumbs (if making the pastry shells for fruit tarts, add the sugar at this time). Mix in the water a little at a time, resulting in a soft ball of dough that leaves the sides of the bowl clean.

Flour a flat surface, place the dough, and begin rolling into a large circle until thin. Using a cookie cutter, cut circles that are a bit bigger than your mini-muffin tin or mini-quiche/tartlet pan. Lay each circle over a mini-pan and press to shape into the molded pan (you may use different shapes if you have them). Bake for 15 minutes or until golden brown (if making for fruit tarts, prick the bottom of the shape before baking). Let the pans cool, and then pry out of the pastry shells and set on a wire rack. You are now ready to add your filling.

Filling

Beat together the eggs, milk, and nutmeg (omit the nutmeg if making fruit tarts). Pour your selected fillings into prepared pastry shells that have been arranged on a cookie sheet. Pour the egg mixture over the fillings, and bake for 20 minutes or until filling is set in the middle.

When choosing a filling, just think of what you enjoy eating, and don't be afraid to get creative. Here are some filling suggestions to try (use about ½ tablespoon of filling per mini-quiche then top with the egg mixture):

- Chopped scallions, lox, cream cheese, and capers
- Shredded provolone cheese, sliced grape tomatoes, and a fresh basil leaf on top
- Sliced mushrooms and shredded Swiss cheese
- Chopped leeks and shredded spiral ham
- Taco meat and shredded jalapeño Monterey Jack cheese

Leafy Pizza Swirls

Makes 1½ dozen

¼ cup provolone cheese, shredded
¼ cup mozzarella cheese, shredded
¼ cup Parmesan cheese
½ yellow onion, diced small
1 garlic clove, diced extra fine
1 pizza dough round (see below)
¼-½ cup extra-virgin olive oil, for brushing
6 cups fresh spinach
1 tablespoon water

Preheat an oven to 350°F. Mix the cheeses, onion, and fresh garlic in a medium bowl. Roll out the dough on a floured surface, stretching to a large rectangle. Brush with a little olive oil. Cook the spinach with 1 tablespoon of water, covered, in the microwave for 3 minutes. Top the dough with the spinach and cheese mixture. Roll up like a jelly roll. Cut into slices ½-inch thick. Place on a baking sheet, 2 inches apart (you may need to use two baking sheets). Brush with additional olive oil, and bake for 15 to 20 minutes or until golden brown. Cool just enough to pick up and eat. Serve immediately. These can be refrigerated or frozen ahead of time, and baked as needed.

Rich Pizza Dough

Makes 1 round

1½ cups self-rising flour
6 tablespoons butter, sliced
⅛ teaspoon salt
½ cup shredded provolone cheese
8 tablespoons milk

In a large bowl, place the flour, butter, and salt. Cut the butter into the flour until it reaches the consistency of gravel. Add the shredded cheese and milk. Mix everything together until you have a smooth ball of dough. Roll out on a floured surface and use as suggested in the recipe.

Spinach Pies

Serves 14-20

1 small yellow onion, chopped extra fine
3 cups fresh spinach
1 tablespoon extra-virgin olive oil
½-¾ cups feta cheese, crumbled
⅛ teaspoon white pepper
1 sheet puff pastry (see page 192)
¼ cup water, for brushing
Sea salt, to taste

Preheat an oven to 400°F. In a large saucepan, sauté the onion and spinach in oil until the spinach is limp and the onion is transparent. Remove from the heat, and add the cheese, pepper, and salt. Roll the pastry into a 12-inch square and cut 14 to 20 squares. Brush the edges with water, place 1 tablespoon of spinach mixture in the center, and form the pastry over the mixture into a triangle shape. Seal the edges using additional water, if necessary, and bake for 14 to 17 minutes or until golden brown (if they brown too fast, brush with water and return to the oven). To keep the squares crispy, remove them from the baking sheet immediately and allow to cool on a wire rack so air circulates on the bottoms and tops. Refrigerate any remaining spinach mixture, and use in an omelet the next morning.

Middle Eastern Meat Pies

Serves 14-20

Several of my old friends in Park Slope (Brooklyn, New York) had Middle Eastern restaurants. The day that my son discovered meat pies was one to remember. Since that day, he can never pass a Middle Eastern restaurant without getting a meat pie. Now that his favorite place has closed, I have been forced to learn how to make them on my own. This is not my friend Elias' recipe, but it is an authentic alternative.

Story by Monica

½ yellow onion, finely chopped
½ teaspoon extra-virgin olive oil
½ pound lean ground beef or bison
½ pound lean ground lamb
¼ cup tomato paste
1 lemon, juiced
1½ teaspoons allspice
1 tablespoon tamarind paste (found in gourmet or Middle Eastern markets)
1 pizza dough round (see page 68)
1 lemon, cut into wedges

Preheat an oven to 400°F. Sauté the onion in olive oil, and add the meats after 2 minutes. Cook until almost fully browned. Stir in the tomato paste, lemon juice, allspice, and tamarind paste. Set aside. Roll out the dough on a floured surface (you may have to roll in two batches). Cut 14 to 20 squares. Brush the edges with water. Fill the centers with 1½ tablespoons of the meat mixture, spreading along the entire bottom and folding into triangles, Arrange the pies on lightly oiled baking sheets. Bake seam-side up for 20 minutes. Remove from the oven, and squeeze juice from the lemon wedges on top. Cool for 5 minutes and serve. This recipe can also be frozen for future use. Place filled, unbaked pies between sheets of waxed paper and freeze.

Homemade Potato Chips

Serves 4-6

Why make homemade potato chips? Because I can. There are always potatoes in the pantry, plus homemade chips are delicious and don't have any preservatives (not to worry: they won't last long, anyway). Season to your own taste and have fun making them with the kids—even grown-up kids like to make them. Make a dip to go along with them and get the party started. My favorite dip is French Onion (see next page).

Story by Monica

1 pound large Idaho or Yukon Gold potatoes
Extra-virgin olive oil spray or canola oil spray, as needed
Salt, to taste

Preheat an oven to 375°F. Wash and skin the potatoes. Dry completely and cut into the thinnest possible slices (ideally using a mandolin slicer). Lightly spray a cookie sheet with cooking spray, and lay out the slices, being careful not to overlap. Lightly spray the slices and dab with a paper towel if any oil pools on the surfaces of the chips. Bake for 10 to 15 minutes, then turn once. Remove any chips that are getting browned too quickly. Bake for another 10 to 15 minutes. Turn out onto a paper towel to blot the oil. Add salt or your favorite flavorings (see note), and serve with your favorite dip or eat as is.

Sprinkle other flavors on the chips, such as onion and garlic powder, Old Bay seasoning, or barbecue-flavored salt.

French Onion Dip

Serves 6-8

1 large onion, finely diced
2 tablespoons extra-virgin olive oil or canola oil
1 tablespoon salted butter
1 small scallion with green left on, finely chopped
1 cup sour cream
1 teaspoon onion powder
1 teaspoon celery salt
1 teaspoon dried parsley
Dash paprika
⅛ teaspoon mayonnaise

Caramelize the onion in the oil and butter for 20-30 minutes, stirring frequently. Transfer to a medium-sized bowl. Refrigerate to chill. Once cooled sufficiently, add the caramelized onions and scallions to the sour cream, mix, and then add in the dry ingredients, mixing well. Mix in the mayonnaise. Chill before serving with your homemade potato chips. If desired, garnish with a bit of scallions.

Peanut Butter Balls

Nora Rooney *(Raleigh, NC)*
Makes 2 dozen

> This was the first recipe that I ever requested from someone, and it was shared with me by my friend's mother when I was just a child. I asked for the recipe after I had these peanut butter balls at her house at Christmas. I have been making them ever since, and everyone always loves them.

Peanut Butter Balls

1½ cups peanut butter
1 stick butter
2 teaspoons vanilla
½ teaspoon salt
¾ to 1 box 10-X powdered confectioners' sugar

Dipping Chocolate

¼ cake (1 oz.) paraffin
1 (12 oz.) package chocolate chips

Peanut Butter Balls

Mix all the ingredients and chill. Roll into 1-inch balls.

Dipping Chocolate

Melt the paraffin in a double-boiler on low heat; add chocolate chips. Dip the balls and place on waxed paper. Chill, and then serve.

Salmon in Puff Pastry

Serves 8

2 cups tiny shrimp, shelled
¼ cup scallions, including greens, finely sliced
2 tablespoons salted butter
2 tablespoons fresh lemon juice
1 pound salmon, skinned
1 sheet puff pastry (see page 192)
1 egg, beaten
1 tablespoon water

Preheat an oven to 350°F. Using a skillet, sauté the shrimp and scallions in butter on low heat. Just before the shrimp turn pink, add the lemon juice. Then turn off heat and place the salmon on top to steam, covered, for 10 minutes. Place the puff pastry on a baking sheet. Remove the salmon from the shrimp mixture and set aside. Pour the shrimp mixture into the center of the puff pastry, and place the whole salmon on top. Create an egg mixture by combining the beaten egg and water. Wrap the sides of the pastry up over the salmon and seal the seams with the egg mixture. Place seam-side down on a baking sheet and brush with the remaining egg mixture. Bake for 25 minutes or until golden brown. Cool on a baking rack for 10 to 15 minutes. Slice into 8 to 10 slices and serve on a platter with Dijon mustard for dipping.

Almond Meringue Torte with Lemon Curd and Hazelnut

Nora Rooney *(Raleigh, NC)*
Serves 10-12

> This is an outstanding recipe, and I have never eaten anything like it before or since. I first had this almond meringue torte at my friend Marla's baby shower, where it was made by my friend Catherine from Monroe, North Carolina. I think that it is one of the most delicious things I have ever eaten. It is best served close to room temperature, so I recommend that you take it out of the refrigerator about twenty minutes before eating it. For Valentine's Day, I adapted the recipe to make it into the shape of a heart for my boyfriend Bill. He really loved that extra special touch.

French Buttercream
10 tablespoons sugar
2½ tablespoons water
4 egg yolks
1 cup unsalted butter
2 tablespoons vanilla extract or 2 tablespoons fruit brandy

Almond Meringue
⅓ cup sifted cornstarch
¼ cup finely ground blanched almonds
3 egg whites, room temperature
1 teaspoon vanilla (or more to taste)
⅛ teaspoon cream of tartar
⅛ teaspoon salt
¾ cup sugar

Torte
¾ cup lemon curd (see note)
French Buttercream
1½ cups finely chopped toasted hazelnuts/almonds

French Buttercream

Place the sugar and water in a saucepan, and bring to a boil over medium-high heat. Boil until the sugar dissolves, stirring once or twice. Beat the egg yolks in a mixer bowl until blended. Add the hot sugar syrup in a fine stream, beating constantly until blended. Beat for 5 minutes until thick and pale yellow. Let cool. Gradually add the unsalted butter, beating until blended. Beat in vanilla extract/fruit brandy. Set aside or store in the refrigerator (see note).

Almond Meringue

Preheat an oven to 325°F. Line two baking sheets with nonstick parchment paper. Draw a 9-inch circle on each sheet. Mix the cornstarch and almonds in a bowl. Beat the egg whites, vanilla, cream of tartar, and salt in a mixer bowl until soft peaks form. Gradually add the sugar, beating constantly until stiff peaks form. Fold in the almond mixture. Spread half the meringue inside each circle and smooth with a spatula. As an alternative, you can place the meringue mixture into a pastry tube fitted with a ⅜-inch tip and pipe it into the circles. Bake one meringue at a time for 25 minutes or until dry and slightly crisp. Using a spatula, transfer the meringues to a flat surface to cool.

Torte

Arrange one meringue on a serving platter. Spread with the lemon curd. Top with the second meringue. Spread some of the French Buttercream over the sides.

Hold the torte from the bottom over a large pan, and gently pat the hazelnuts/almonds over the sides. Return the torte to the serving platter. Spread the top with the remaining French Buttercream. Chill for several hours before serving (or store in the refrigerator).

You can make the meringue up to 1 week in advance. Simply wrap it in plastic and store in the refrigerator until ready to use. For a tart flavor, try adding real lemon juice to the lemon curd.

French Bread

Serves 4-6

Makes 1 loaf

1 package active dry yeast
1 cup warm water
1 teaspoon salt
2 teaspoons sugar
3 cups all-purpose flour
Cornmeal

Preheat an oven to 425°F. Dissolve the yeast in water and salt. Mix in the sugar and flour. Knead until the dough becomes a ball. Flour your hands and remove the dough from the bowl, placing it in a greased bowl and turning to coat. Cover with a tea towel and let rise until doubled (about an hour). Remove from the bowl, punch the dough down, and shape into a 12-inch log. Brush with water. Cut several slashes into the top of the dough. Place onto a cookie sheet, lightly sprinkle with cornmeal, and set the cookie sheet in the center rack of your oven. On the bottom rack of your oven, place a baking pan filled halfway with water. Bake for 25 to 30 minutes or until lightly browned (the outside should be crispy). You may double this recipe to use for making more bread for future use.

To freeze bread for future use, wrap in plastic wrap, and then in aluminum foil. Place into a freezer bag and suck out all of the air with a straw. Freeze. When ready to use, defrost on the counter or remove all the plastic, and rewrap in aluminum foil. Warm in the oven and use immediately.

Tangy Cheddar Cheese with Port Wine

Serves 6

8 ounces sharp cheddar cheese, shredded
⅓ cup light cream
3 tablespoons port wine
¼ teaspoon Hungarian paprika
¼ teaspoon hot sauce

Mix all the ingredients together until smooth. Place in a decorative bowl, and serve with crackers or toasted French bread (see previous page).

Creamy Shrimp Dip

Serves 6

1 cup cooked shrimp, finely chopped
1 (8 oz.) package cream cheese
⅛ cup heavy cream
1 tablespoon mayonnaise
2 scallions with greens, finely chopped
1 teaspoon lemon juice
⅛ teaspoon Hungarian paprika
¼ teaspoon powdered garlic

Mix all the ingredients together until smooth. Serve with toasted French bread (see previous page).

Part IV

ENTRÉES

ENTRÉES

Dinnertime can sometimes be difficult to plan. Every night does not lend itself to an extravagant meal with a crisp, white linen tablecloth and napkins (although, in my dreams, I try to accomplish that as often as possible). Nonetheless, whether or not you are in a rush, you can always find time on the weekends or on your days off to plan your meals for the rest of the week. You can also take this time to set out your everyday dinnerware, and place fresh flowers or autumn foliage on your dining table for the next week. Little touches like this will brighten everyone's mood at dinnertime, no matter how busy their day has been.

On some nights, between working late, attending sports practices, finishing homework, and enjoying hobbies, a delicious Wholesome Turkey Pie (page 99) or Fall Farm Stand Quiche (page 83) served with a salad is just what everyone needs. Savory pies can be made ahead of time so, if everyone is coming home at a different hour—and we all experience those evenings—they can simply slice off a hefty helping and enjoy.

In the colder months, a traditional English meat pie like the Guinness® Meat Pie (page 92) is extremely hearty and satisfying. For the warmer weather, a light New England Seafood Quiche (page 87) serves the same purpose. You can make your own dough for your pie crusts ahead of time and freeze them for later use, or pile your delicious ingredients into a store-bought crust. Although some nights may require the convenience of using store-bought dough, making your own affords you the opportunity to control what kind of fat you will be using, in case you opt for a healthy variation.

Pie crusts using gluten-free or vegan ingredients are also becoming very popular in many households, even if you are not on a restricted diet. Cutting fat and calories is becoming the norm for many families, as we strive to stay on the path to better health. Of course, the important thing to remember is we can still eat our favorite foods in moderation. You know when you are overdoing it, so put on the brakes, eat smart and balanced meals, and you will find that you won't have to limit your menu quite so much. In my home, we never serve pizza or a savory pie without a sufficient helping of fresh leafy green salad or a vegetable such as broccoli or asparagus that will assist in metabolizing your food more efficiently.

As always, dinnertime is a special time, because it is a chance to unwind and relax at the end of the day, savor good food, and get ready to do it all again tomorrow.

Fall Farm Stand Quiche

Serves 8

Pie Crust

2 cups flour

1½ tablespoons cornmeal

½ teaspoon baking powder

¼ teaspoon baking soda

¼ teaspoon salt

½ cup butter

¼ cup buttermilk

Assembly

2 (9-inch) pie crusts

1½ tablespoons cornmeal

1 large purple eggplant, roasted and diced

3 tablespoons extra-virgin olive oil

1 large yellow onion, finely chopped

4 cloves garlic, minced

1 large red pepper, diced

1 large green pepper, diced

1 large zucchini, diced

1 large yellow squash, diced

3-4 large beefsteak tomatoes

1 teaspoon dried oregano or 1 tablespoon fresh (leaves only), finely chopped

2 teaspoons dried thyme or 4 tablespoons fresh (leaves only), finely chopped

1 teaspoon dried parsley or 2 tablespoons fresh (leaves only), finely chopped

¼ cup mozzarella cheese, shredded

4 eggs, beaten

1 cup cream

½ cup Parmesan cheese

Pie Crust

In a medium-sized bowl, mix the flour, cornmeal, baking powder, baking soda, and salt. Cut in the butter with your fingertips until the dough resembles coarse meal. Add buttermilk, and knead until a ball forms. Wrap the dough in plastic and chill for 1 hour.

Assembly

Preheat an oven to 350°F. Line the two pie plates with the dough. Sprinkle the dough with cornmeal. Set aside. Roast the eggplant (see note), dice, and set aside. Sauté the onion in olive oil for 2 minutes, add in the garlic, and cook for another minute. Add in the vegetables (including the eggplant), stir, and add in herbs. Cook for about 5 minutes. Remove from the stove and mix in the mozzarella cheese. Pour the mixture into two pie crusts. Mix the eggs and cream, and then pour half of the mixture into each pie crust. Cover with Parmesan cheese, and bake for 45 minutes or until the crust is golden and the cheese is golden brown. Cool on a rack for 10 minutes before cutting.

How to Roast a Whole Eggplant

It is easier than you think to roast an eggplant. Prick several holes in the eggplant, brush it completely with extra-virgin olive oil, and bake for 1 hour at 350°F.

Rustic Garden Tomato Pie

Serves 6-8

> Every summer, we are blessed with a bounty of fresh tomatoes and herbs from the garden. Coming up with new recipes to use all of our vegetables can become a tasty challenge. By exchanging recipes with friends and trolling through cookbooks, I usually find something new every season and make it my own. This recipe is one that I have come across that has become a great hit.
>
> *Story by Monica*

Herb Crust

1 egg
1 cup cooked brown rice
½ cup grated cheddar cheese
½ teaspoon butter
¼ teaspoon dried lemon thyme

Filling

8 plum tomatoes, sliced
9 cloves garlic, roasted
1½ tablespoons extra-virgin olive oil
8 sprigs lemon thyme
8 asparagus spears, trimmed to half their length and cooked
½ cup pitted black olives, sliced
2 ounces feta cheese, crumbled
3 eggs
¼ cup light cream

Crust

Preheat an oven to 400°F. Beat the egg, and mix with the rest of the ingredients. Grease a 10-inch quiche dish, and press the mixture on the bottom and up the sides (as you would for a cookie crumb crust). Bake for 15 minutes. Cool on a wire rack.

Filling

Cut the tomatoes in half and roast with the garlic on a lightly greased (using olive oil) cookie sheet. Lightly brush with additional olive oil, and bake for 30 minutes. After removing from the oven, remove the garlic skin. Set the tomatoes and garlic aside. Arrange the tomatoes, garlic, lemon thyme sprigs, asparagus, olives, and feta cheese on the crust in a decorative pattern. Whisk the eggs and cream, and pour over the tomato surface. Bake at 350°F for 1 hour or until the center appears set. Let rest for 10 minutes before slicing.

New England Seafood Quiche

Serves 8

2 cups spinach, washed and chopped
1 cup kale, washed and chopped
2 tablespoons water, divided
1 pound cooked shrimp
½ pound haddock, cooked and cubed
4 scallions, with greens, sliced
3 tablespoons butter
4 eggs
2 cups heavy cream
1 teaspoon salt
½ teaspoon mixed peppercorns, ground
1 (9-inch) deep-dish pie crust (see page 191)

Preheat an oven to 350°F. Steam the spinach in 1 tablespoon of water for about 1 minute. Steam the kale in 1 tablespoon of water for about 4 minutes. Mix together the shrimp, haddock, spinach, kale, and scallions, and dot with butter. In a separate bowl, mix the eggs with cream, salt, and pepper. Pour the fish mixture into the pie shell, and then add the egg mixture. Bake for 45 minutes or until firm in the middle.

Best-Ever Broccoli and Cheddar Quiche

Serves 8

This is my mom's favorite quiche. It is full of vegetables and cheese, without any meat. She could literally eat this every day, and never tire of it.

Story by Monica

1 (9-inch) deep-dish pie crust (see page 191)
1 cup broccoli florets, cooked and chopped
¾ cup cheddar cheese, shredded
3 eggs
1½ cups half-and-half
⅛ teaspoon mixed peppercorns, ground

Preheat an oven to 375°F. Line a pie plate with the pie crust. Place alternating layers of broccoli and cheese until all is used. Beat the eggs, and mix with half-and-half and pepper, then pour over the broccoli and cheese. Bake for 30 to 40 minutes or until the center is firm and the crust is lightly browned. Let sit for 5 minutes before serving as individual slices.

Make a spinach and Swiss cheese quiche by switching out the broccoli and cheddar. Switch out the peppercorns for nutmeg.

Try a Greek-inspired quiche by switching out the cheddar cheese for feta, and replacing the peppercorns with nutmeg.

Country Potato Quiche

Serves 8

> My brother makes this quiche for his wife, who prefers meat
> over vegetables. It is packed with pungent flavors, which are
> just right for a delightful meal.
>
> *Story by Monica*

1 (9-inch) deep-dish pie crust (see page 191)
6 small red potatoes, skinned, parboiled, drained, and sliced
4 eggs
⅔ cup heavy cream
6 slices bacon, cooked, drained, and chopped small
4 slices Virginia ham, chopped
1 cup cheddar cheese, shredded
½ teaspoon fresh basil, finely chopped
½ teaspoon fresh parsley, finely chopped
1 teaspoon fresh chives, finely chopped

Preheat an oven to 350°F. Layer the potatoes in the pie crust. Beat
the eggs and cream until well-blended. Combine all the remaining
ingredients (except the chives), stir into the egg mixture, and pour
over the potatoes. Sprinkle the chives over the whole surface. Bake
for 30 to 40 minutes or until the center is firm and the crust edges
are light brown. Let sit for 5 minutes before serving as individual
slices.

Turn this into an Italian quiche by switching out the bacon and
ham for salami and pepperoni. Use ½ cup of shredded provolone
and ½ cup of shredded mozzarella instead of the cheeses listed
above. Omit the chives, and sprinkle a little dried oregano and
Parmesan cheese over the top.

Beef Wellington

Serves 4-6

This recipe may look difficult, but if you prepare your puff pastry beforehand (see page 192) or are using a frozen store-bought product, this dish is really simple to make, and is a real show-stopper. Everyone will be impressed.

Story by Monica

1 beef tenderloin (2 to 2½ pounds)
½ teaspoon sea salt
½ teaspoon freshly ground black pepper
1 egg
1 tablespoon water
1 tablespoon butter
2 cups mushrooms, finely chopped
½ cup shallots, finely chopped
2 tablespoons goose liver pâté
All-purpose flour, as needed
1 sheet puff pastry (see page 192)

Gravy (optional)
¾ cup dry Madeira wine
16 ounces beef stock
2 stalks celery, trimmed and halved
1 small whole onion
1 clove garlic, pressed
2 tablespoons cornstarch or other thickener
Salt and pepper, to taste

Easy Sauce (optional)
½ cup prepared white horseradish
¼ cup prepared mayonnaise

Preheat the oven to 425°F. Place the beef into a lightly greased roasting pan. Season with salt and pepper. Roast for 35 to 50 minutes, depending on how well-done you like your meat. Cover the pan and refrigerate for 1 hour. In the meantime, beat the egg and water in a small bowl with a fork. Heat the butter over medium-high heat. Then add the mushrooms and shallots, and cook until the mushrooms are tender and all the liquid is evaporated. Add in the pâté and stir until combined. Sprinkle a flat surface with flour. Place your pastry, and roll it into a rectangle just wider than your meat. Brush with the egg mixture. Spoon the mushroom and pâté mixture onto the pastry sheet, leaving 1 inch from the edge on all sides. Place the beef in the center of the mushroom mixture. Fold the pastry over the beef and press to seal, using some water, if necessary. Place seam-side down onto a baking sheet. Tuck the ends under to seal. Brush the pastry with the egg mixture. Bake for 25 minutes or until the pastry is golden brown. Let rest before serving. Cut into slices and serve on its own or with Gravy or Easy Sauce.

Gravy (optional)

Combine ½ cup of wine with the stock, celery, onion, and garlic. Boil and then simmer for 30 minutes. In a separate bowl, combine the remaining wine and cornstarch. Add to the simmering pot, and simmer down until your desired thickness. Salt and pepper to taste.

Easy Sauce (optional)

Mix all the ingredients and chill. Serve at the table in a lovely bowl with a small serving spoon.

Guinness® Meat Pie

Serves 8

I had my first authentic English meat pie at a pub in Oxford, England, with my husband's brother and his wife during one of our vacations. My sister-in-law had gone to school there, and knew all the best places to eat. This version is reminiscent of a thick savory pie that I enjoyed there, and have never forgotten.

Story by Monica

Simple Pastry

(Makes two 9-inch crusts)

3 cups flour

1 teaspoon salt

1 teaspoon baking powder

⅔-1 cup shortening

½ cup cold water

Meat Pie

2 pounds filet mignon, cubed

1 tablespoon all-purpose flour

3 tablespoons butter

½ pound bacon, chopped

5 yellow onions, finely chopped

¼ pound fresh mushrooms, sliced

1 (12 oz.) bottle Guinness® Irish stout

1 tablespoon fresh parsley, chopped

1 tablespoon raisins

1 teaspoon brown sugar

Simple Pastry

Sift the flour, salt, and baking powder together. Cut in the shortening. Add water. Mix, shape into a ball, and then cut in half and roll out two crusts.

Meat Pie

Preheat an oven to 325°F. Dredge the filet mignon in flour. Heat the bacon in butter until it sizzles. Stir in the filet mignon, and sauté for 15 minutes or until browned. Transfer the mixture to a large baking dish and set aside. Using the same skillet, cook the onions and mushrooms over medium heat for approximately 10 minutes. Mix with the filet mignon mixture, then stirring in Guinness®, parsley, raisins, and brown sugar. Cover tightly with aluminum foil. Bake in the oven for 2 to 3 hours or until the gravy has thickened, stirring occasionally. Remove from the oven and increase the temperature to 400°F. Place one Simple Pastry crust on the bottom of a 9-inch deep-dish pie plate and bake for about 10 minutes. Remove from the oven and spoon in the meat mixture. Cover with the second crust and seal the edges tightly against the bottom crust. Bake for about 10 to 15 minutes or until the crust is golden brown.

Old-Fashioned Savory Meat Pie

Serves 8

I had this pie when I was in England, and have recreated it to replicate an old-fashioned take on chicken pot pie. This will be less juicy and more solid, similar to a fruit pie. The carrots, celery, and parsley are my own additions, and are optional, as many of the traditional meat pies that I tasted while traveling didn't contain vegetables. In earlier times, fresh vegetables may not have been readily accessible, and the contents of the pies would have come from what was available on the farm. I add vegetables to just about anything that I make for a healthier take on an heirloom recipe.

Story by Monica

Pie Crust
2 cups all-purpose flour
½ cup shortening
¼ cup water

Meat Pie
2-3 cups cooked chicken, cubed
¼ cup bacon, cooked and coarsely chopped
¼ cup carrots, shredded (optional)
¼ cup celery, shredded (optional)
2 eggs
1 cup chicken gravy
1 tablespoon dried parsley
1 egg white

Pie Crust

Measure the flour into a large bowl. Cut in the shortening, working until well-blended. Make a depression in the center and add water, blending rapidly. Divide in half and roll out two crusts. Line a pie plate with one. Trim strips of dough from around the edges of the pie plate and set aside for use later. Reserve the second crust for the top.

Meat Pie

Preheat an oven to 375°F. Layer the chicken and bacon in the pie crust, then layering in the carrots and celery. Put the trimmed scraps of pie crust around the edges. Beat the eggs, and mix with gravy and parsley. Pour over the meat. Cover with the second crust. Brush the crust with egg white. Prick holes in the top to vent. Secure the edges with a fork. Bake for 40 minutes or until the top is browned.

Fast Frittata

Christine Gable, www.QuickMealHelp.com *(Lititz, PA)*
Serves 4

> This fast frittata recipe is an easy way to stretch eggs into dinner (and use up those extra veggies in the refrigerator). Try substituting two to three tablespoons of salsa for the tomatoes for a spicy Mexican twist, or add some cooked crumbled bacon to boost the protein.

2 tablespoons vegetable oil
1 medium onion, minced
3 cups vegetables (such as broccoli, cauliflower, carrots, or peppers), frozen or freshly chopped
1 cup diced or crushed tomatoes, with juice
1 teaspoon dried oregano
1 teaspoon dried basil
¼ teaspoon adobo or garlic salt
¼ teaspoon black pepper
6 eggs, lightly beaten
½ cup shredded cheese (such as cheddar or mozzarella)

Preheat an oven to 375°F. Spray a pie plate or 9- x 13-inch baking dish with vegetable oil spray, and set aside. Add oil to a heavy skillet over medium heat; add onion and sauté for 1 to 2 minutes. Add vegetables, tomatoes, herbs, adobo, and pepper. Sauté for 3 to 4 minutes. Spread the vegetable mixture in the bottom of the oiled baking dish and pour the eggs on top. Sprinkle the cheese on top. Bake for 20 to 24 minutes or until golden brown.

Shades of Red Goat Cheese Pizza

Serves 4-6

⅛ cup semolina flour
1 pizza dough (see page 68)
4 tablespoons extra-virgin olive oil, divided
5 red onions, sliced extra thin
½ pound red peppers, roasted and sliced thin
1 cup grape tomatoes, cut in half
½ cups large, ripe red olives, pitted and sliced in thirds
2 ounces feta cheese
12 sage leaves, chopped
⅛ teaspoon black pepper, freshly ground
1/16 teaspoon sea salt

Roll out the pizza dough on a surface sprinkled with semolina. Prepare the topping by first caramelizing the onions in 3 tablespoons of the olive oil (this should take about 30 minutes). Preheat an oven to 415°F. Place the rolled dough onto a round pizza stone, brush lightly with the remaining olive oil, and alternately top with onions, peppers, tomatoes, olives, and cheese. Sprinkle with sage, pepper, and sea salt. Bake for 25 minutes. Let sit for 5 minutes before cutting into slices and serving.

Ham and Cheese Soufflé

Mary Carlin (*East Meadow, NY*)
Serves 4

> My mother-in-law Mary liked to be daring, and was one of the few people who I had met who ever braved the soufflé. She often made this one for using leftover ham from a previous meal. My husband used this recipe from Mary's recipe box for us at home...he was fearless, too.
>
> *Story by Monica*

4 tablespoons butter
4 tablespoons flour
1 cup milk
¼ teaspoon dry mustard
Dash cayenne pepper
1 cup sharp cheddar cheese, shredded
½ cup cooked ham, ground
3 egg yolks, well-beaten
3 egg whites
½ teaspoon cream of tartar
Salt, to taste

Preheat an oven to 350°F. Make a thick white sauce using the butter, flour, and milk. Add mustard, cayenne, and salt. Heat until thickened, then stir in the cheese and ham. Remove from the heat. Stir in the egg yolks. Beat the egg whites with cream of tartar until stiff, then fold the cheese mixture into the egg white mixture. Pour into a 1½-quart ungreased casserole. Set in a pan of water 1-inch deep. Bake until puffed and golden brown (about 50 minutes). Serve immediately.

Wholesome Turkey Pie

Serves 6

Savory Pastry

1 cup flour

½ teaspoon dried parsley

½ teaspoon celery seed

½ teaspoon sea salt

½ teaspoon Hungarian paprika

⅓ cup plus 1 tablespoon butter

2 tablespoons cold water

Pie

1 savory pastry

½ cup mushrooms, thinly sliced

¼ cup butter

¼ cup whole-wheat flour

¼ teaspoon sea salt

1 ounce turkey (or chicken) stock

1 cup light cream

½ pound vegetarian sausage, crumbled

2 cups cooked turkey breast, shredded

Savory Pastry

Mix the flour, parsley, celery seed, salt, and paprika. Cut the butter into slices and cut into the flour mixture. Sprinkle with water 1 tablespoon at a time until the dough is thoroughly mixed and clears the sides of the bowl. Shape into a ball and roll out to about ⅛-inch thick on a floured surface. Cut into six rounds to place over ramekins 1½ inches in diameter (you can also make a savory pastry with different herbs or spices to create a flavor to complement your filling).

Pie

Preheat an oven to 425°F. Sauté the mushrooms in butter until tender. Stir in the flour and salt, and cook over low heat until about to boil. Stir in the stock and cream, and heat to boiling, stirring constantly about 1 more minute. Divide the sausage crumbles and turkey in six (1½ cup) ramekins and pour in the sauce. Cut the pastry into ¼-inch-thick rounds big enough to cover each ramekin. Press down to seal. Bake until the sauce is bubbling.

Shrimp Surprise Soufflé

Mary Carlin *(East Meadow, NY)*
Serves 6

> With the exception of the milk-egg mixture, this dish can be assembled in advance and left in the refrigerator. Just before baking, add in the milk-egg mixture. This yields five to six servings, but my mother-in-law usually made two of these at a time to serve everyone generously.

8 slices white bread (see page 12)
Butter, as needed
½-¾ cup shrimp
2 cups sharp cheddar cheese, shredded
2 cups milk
3 eggs, slightly beaten
½ teaspoon salt
¼ teaspoon dry mustard
Dash pepper

Preheat an oven to 350°F. Spread the bread with butter. Cut in 1-inch squares, leaving the crusts on. Arrange half in a shallow greased baking dish or 9-inch pie plate. Cover well with half of the shrimp and half of the cheese. Add the remaining bread cubes, the remaining shrimp, and the remaining cheese. Carefully pour the milk-egg mixture, salt, mustard, and pepper over the bread and cheese. Bake for 40 minutes or until the custard is set. Serve immediately.

Thanksgiving Oyster Pie

Mary Carlin *(East Meadow, NY)*
Serves 6

> The traditional Thanksgiving feast said to have occurred between the Pilgrims and the Native Americans included oysters. This dish is served during the Thanksgiving season. My mother-in-law, Mary, used to make several oyster dishes; this is one of them.

1 quart oysters, shucked in their own liquid
½ cup light cream
¹⁄₁₆ teaspoon ground mace
⅛ teaspoon freshly ground black pepper
2 cups crumbled crackers
½ cup butter, melted

Preheat the oven to 350°F. Drain the oysters, reserving the liquid. Add the cream to the liquid to make 1½ cups. Add mace and pepper to the cracker crumbs, then pour the butter over the crumbs, mixing well. Layer in one-third of the crumbs into an 8-inch pie plate, followed by a layer of oysters, another layer of crumbs, and a final layer of oysters. Pour the oyster liquid mixture over the pie and top with the remaining crumbs. Bake for 30 to 40 minutes until the center is set. Serve immediately. Do not reheat leftovers.

Crab Quiche

Mary Carlin *(East Meadow, NY)*
Serves 4-8

This dish can also be used as an appetizer. My mother-in-law, Mary, used to make two at a time, and freeze the second one for a future meal. The food was always homemade at her house. She was known for her dinner parties, large and small, where she would always take the time to prepare her guests' favorite dishes.

1 (6 oz.) package frozen snow crab or 3 ounces crabmeat plus 3 ounces chopped shrimp
1 (9-inch) pie shell, unbaked
¼ cup Swiss cheese, shredded
⅓ cup minced onion
1 tablespoon parsley, minced
1 tablespoon sherry wine
⅛ teaspoon leaf tarragon
3 eggs
1 cup half-and-half or light cream
½ teaspoon salt

Thaw, drain thoroughly, and then coarsely chop the crabmeat (or crabmeat and shrimp). Bake the pie shell in a 425°F oven for 10 minutes; do not brown. Sprinkle the cheese over the bottom of the partially baked pie shell. Toss the crab lightly with onion, parsley, sherry, and tarragon; arrange in a layer over the cheese. With a whisk, beat the eggs, half-and-half, and salt just to mix; pour gradually over the crab mixture. Reduce the heat to 325°F, and bake for 45 to 50 minutes or until set. Let stand for 5 minutes before cutting into wedges to serve.

Mexican Enchilada Pie

Serves 8

1 yellow onion, chopped

1 clove garlic, minced

5-6 mushrooms, sliced

1 small green pepper, chopped

2 large ears corn, shucked, cooked, and cut off the cob

1½ cups cooked black beans

1½ cups stewed tomatoes

1 tablespoon chili powder

1 teaspoon ground cumin

½ cup red wine (such as Bordeaux)

6-8 corn tortillas

½ cup Monterey Jack cheese, shredded

½ cup cheddar cheese, shredded

½ cup ricotta cheese

½ cup plain yogurt

Extra-virgin olive oil, as needed

Black olives, to garnish

Preheat an oven to 350°F. Sauté the onion, garlic, mushrooms, green pepper, and corn in oil in a large skillet. Add beans, tomatoes, spices, and wine, and simmer for 30 minutes. Place a layer of tortillas in an oiled 9-inch deep-dish casserole. Top with a layer of sauce, grated cheese, and ricotta-yogurt mix. Repeat the layers. Top with the ricotta-yogurt mixture, and garnish with olives. Bake for 20 minutes. Let sit for 5 minutes before slicing.

Socca

Marlisa Brown, M.S., R.D., C.D.E. *(Bay Shore, NY)*
Recipe first published in *Gluten-Free, Hassle-Free: A Simple, Sane, Dietician-Approved Program for Eating Your Way Back to Health*
Serves 4

> Socca are traditionally found in Nice, France, and northern Italy. Not only are socca quick and easy to make, they also have a fabulous taste and texture.

1 cup chickpea flour
1 cup water
1¼ tablespoons olive oil
½ tablespoon chopped fresh rosemary
½ teaspoon salt
¼ teaspoon pepper
¼ cup onion or shallots, sliced thin (optional)
Gluten-free cooking spray (or vegetable oil), as needed

Mix together the chickpea flour, water, 1 tablespoon of olive oil, rosemary, salt, pepper, and shallots. Let sit for about 30 minutes, covered, at room temperature (the mixture will resemble a thick cream). Preheat an oven to broil. Spray a 9½-inch-round nonstick skillet with cooking spray (or coat with vegetable oil), and heat on a low flame until hot. Pour about ½ cup of batter into the pan and swirl around to coat the pan like a crepe (use a rubber spatula to loosen up the sides). Cook the socca until crispy on one side, and then slide onto a cookie sheet or a pizza pan. Drizzle with ¼ tablespoon of olive oil and brown under the broiler until it just starts to crisp.

Although socca is traditionally made on a different type of pan and in a much hotter oven, cooking as directed above reduces the fat by half, and is an easier alternative for home cooks. Socca can be used as a flatbread to use with dips, or it can be topped with any of your favorite toppings. If you wish to add toppings, broil the socca until it just starts to crisp, and then lightly sprinkle with cheese, tomato, or any other favorites. Put back under the broiler to finish. Keep the toppings light so you don't drown out the flavor of the socca.

Buffalo Chicken Cupcakes
Serves 10

> As soon as I sampled this unusual confection at a Super Bowl
> Party, I just had to make it myself. I love bleu cheese and Buffalo
> chicken wings, so I asked for the recipe, and the rest is history.
> It is an acquired taste, but well worth it.
>
> *Story by Monica*

Cupcakes
½ cup hot sauce
¼ cup butter
½ cup bleu cheese, crumbled
1 cup light brown sugar
¼ cup plus 2 tablespoons sour cream
1 egg
1 cup flour
1¼ teaspoons baking soda

Bleu Cheese Frosting
2 ounces bleu cheese, crumbled
½ cup butter, room temperature
2 cups confectioners' sugar

Buffalo Chicken Topper
2 cooked chicken breasts, shredded
8 ounces hot pepper sauce
½ cup butter
2 tablespoons white vinegar
1 teaspoon garlic powder
6 celery sticks, trimmed and cut into strips

Cupcakes

Preheat an oven to 350°F. In a medium-sized saucepan on medium-high heat, heat the hot sauce and butter until the butter is melted. Add the bleu cheese, and mix until melted. Remove from the heat and mix in the brown sugar. In a small bowl, whisk together the sour cream and egg. Cool down the hot sauce and mix with the sour cream mixture. In a small bowl, sift the flour and baking soda. Combine the flour mixture with the hot sauce mixture. Fill cupcake liners ¾ full. Bake for 20 minutes or until a skewer inserted in the center comes out clean.

Bleu Cheese Frosting

Beat the bleu cheese until smooth. Add butter, and mix for 3 to 4 minutes. Mix in the confectioners' sugar a little at a time. Ice the cupcakes.

Buffalo Chicken Topper

Shred the chicken, and mix with the hot pepper sauce, butter, vinegar, and garlic powder. Heat for 5 minutes in a medium saucepan. Spoon ½ teaspoon into the center of the iced cupcake, top with a celery stick, and serve.

Pizza Rustica

Jeannine Rocco *(Sayville, NY)*
Makes 4 pies

> I met Jeannine at Blanca's Spa in Sayville, New York, the day before Easter. She had made these Easter meat pies (also called Pizza Rustica) to bring to her traditional Italian family dinner the next day. As we leisurely chatted, she shared this recipe with me from memory as I transcribed it. It uses several kinds of meats and cheeses, is extremely rich, and is usually served during holidays.
>
> *Story by Monica*

2 pizza dough rounds (see page 68)
2 pounds whole milk ricotta
1 pound mozzarella
1 cup Parmesan cheese
¼ pound soft provolone
¼ pound prosciutto
¼ pound sopresetta
¼ pound ham
½-1 pound sweet sausage, out of casing and cooked
5-6 eggs
1 egg white, beaten with 1 tablespoon water

Preheat an oven to 350°F. Grease a pie plate. Chop and combine all the meats and cheeses. Place the bottom crust in the pie plate and fill with the mixed meats and cheeses. Cover with the second pie crust, and brush with an egg white wash. Bake for 1 hour or until golden brown. Remove and let settle for 10 minutes before cutting.

Indian-Influenced Shepherd's Pie

Serves 4

1 onion, diced

1 pound ground lamb

2 cloves garlic, minced

½ teaspoon cinnamon

½ teaspoon coriander

¼ teaspoon turmeric

1 cup carrots, sliced and cooked

2 tablespoons tomato paste

8 ounces beef stock

1 teaspoon flour

2 pounds potatoes, mashed

2 tablespoons butter

Preheat an oven to 350°F. Sauté the onion for 3 minutes. Add the lamb and, when almost browned, the garlic, spices, and carrots. Mix in the tomato paste. Add the stock, simmer for another 5 minutes, turn off the heat, and add the flour to thicken. Transfer to a rectangular baking dish. Spread the mashed potatoes on top, and dot with butter. Bake for 45 to 50 minutes or until bubbling under the potatoes. Let sit for 10 minutes before serving.

Indian Naan Bread

Serves 12

4 cups all-purpose flour
1 teaspoon salt
½ teaspoon baking powder
½ cup yogurt
1 tablespoon sugar
1 egg
4 tablespoons vegetable oil
1 teaspoon nigella seeds (can be purchased in an Indian specialty store)

Sift the flour, salt, and baking powder. In a separate bowl, mix the yogurt, sugar, egg, and 2 tablespoons of oil. Mix with the flour, and knead into a soft dough. Add the rest of the oil, and continue kneading for 5 minutes. Cover with a damp cloth, and allow the dough to rest for 15 minutes. Knead the dough again, then cover and leave for 3 hours. Shortly before baking the naan, preheat your oven to 450 to 475°F. Divide the dough into eight equal balls, and allow to rest for 5 minutes. Sprinkle a baking sheet with nigella seeds, and place in the oven. Roll each ball of dough into an oval and place on the baking sheet. Bake until it puffs up and turns golden brown. Follow with the rest of the balls until the dough is finished. Serve warm.

Spicy Shrimp Dip

Serves 6

2 scallions with green parts, chopped
2 tablespoons extra-virgin olive oil
1 dried red chili
1 fresh green chili, finely chopped
½ teaspoon cumin seeds
½ teaspoon turmeric
1 clove garlic, finely minced
1 inch fresh ginger, skinned and finely chopped
4 curry leaves, crumbled
¾ pound small shrimp
1 tablespoon rice vinegar

Sauté the scallions in olive oil in a large skillet for about 2 minutes. Add the dried red chili. Add the fresh green chili along with the cumin, turmeric, garlic, ginger, and curry leaves. Sauté for another 3 minutes. Add the shrimp, and cook for a few more minutes, then adding in the rice vinegar. Simmer for another 4 to 5 minutes until the shrimp is firm, and the liquid is thickened and mostly absorbed. Serve with naan.

Part V

DESSERTS

DESSERTS

We didn't have nightly desserts in my home when I was growing up. My mom was an exceptional cook, but she didn't bake. Nonetheless, we did know of some excellent bakeries in the old Brooklyn neighborhood, which sold some of my family's favorites, such as delicious Lemon Ricotta Cookies (page 164), black and white cakes, and Rugelach (page 169). We usually indulged in those sweets at Sunday breakfast after church.

It wasn't until I married my husband that desserts became a regular tradition, and I enjoyed many different varieties home-made by my mother-in-law. In turn, my son, Matthew, now regularly asks for dessert, and I've had to scramble throughout the years to get with the program and have something ready to serve.

Thanks to my son, I learned how to make cupcakes. I had never made them until he was in elementary school, and it was part of "Mom 101" to make twenty-four perfect cupcakes for a class birthday party. Since I had only cooked and baked from scratch using fresh pumpkin or fruit and very little sugar, mixes with over-sugared icings were out of the question, and I had to search out the perfect recipe for Vanilla Cupcakes (page 124). After I had become a widowed mom, between working full-time, helping with homework, making dinner, and getting my son to bed, my cupcake making began at about 10 p.m. the night before they were due. With cookbook in hand and flour sprinkled everywhere, I finally succeeded in making a decent batch, and was thankful that birthdays only came once a year. I eventually broadened my knowledge, and even began making them more often, decorating them using seasonal themes.

Now, you can find cupcake shops opening up all over town and in shopping malls. Cupcakes have made it to the big-time. They're the perfect individual serving size, making them great for gatherings, because they are compact and easy to handle. Cupcakes have even been used to create the illusion of a wedding cake using cake stands and platforms in dramatic sculptural designs befitting the big day.

Like the bridal gown featured at the end of a fashion show, both spectacular and one-of-a-kind, the traditional wedding cake still maintains its place as the ultimate in cake design and decoration. Multi-tiered and uniquely decorated to suit each bride and groom's dream wedding theme, wedding cakes will never go out of style. My wedding cake in 1977 was supposed to be a three-tiered Junior's strawberry cheesecake, which I had designed with the manager a year before my wedding. However, a week before the wedding, I called regarding delivery, only to find that they could not fulfill the order because they no longer made wedding cakes. I was absolutely crushed, and scrambled to find another unique cake for the most important day of my life. Fortunately, I lived nearby a traditional Italian neighborhood in Brooklyn that had old-fashioned bakeries on every corner. I had the brilliant idea of having an Italian Cassata Cream Cake (page 120), which would be filled entirely with cannoli cream and built into a three-tiered wedding cake. The baker, who spoke very little English, looked at me with my pleading expression and agreed to my request. On my special day, I had my cake and ate it, too.

Nowadays, I am told that Red Velvet Cake (page 117) is the "go-to" cake for weddings. So, I have found the perfect recipe and point-by-point procedure to assist you in making your own wedding cake.

Whether you are baking a nice dessert for your family to enjoy after dinner or a special-occasion cake, you will find that the extra effort is worth it every time. Your children will always remember licking the spoon used for the icing, and think of you when they start to bake with their own kids. Your mom will appreciate that you made her favorite Hawaiian Carrot Cake (page 136) for her birthday. Your Chocolate Silk Cake with Candied Cranberries (page 171) will likely be the first to go at the buffet table. Homemade desserts are a very sweet way of giving, sharing, and passing on your family's traditions.

Manhattan Sweets' Red Velvet Wedding Cake

Werner Simon, Pastry Chef, Manhattan Sweets Boutique Bakery
(Islip, NY)
Serves 75

No book on baking would be complete without a recipe for the ultimate cake: the wedding cake. Manhattan Sweets is an upscale bakery on Long Island, New York, known not only for its delicious bakery items, but also for its fantastic wedding cakes, creatively designed with each bridal couples' particular tastes in mind. They have been kind enough to share their recipe for red velvet cake. The owner Cindy says that red velvet cake is one of the most popular choices today. If you would like to make your own wedding cake, follow these detailed instructions courtesy of Chef Werner. Enjoy!

Story by Monica

Cake

2 pounds cake flour
5 ounces unsweetened cocoa powder
½ ounce baking soda
½ ounce salt
1 pound, 8 ounces butter, softened
2 pounds, 8 ounces sugar
12 eggs
1 pound, 8 ounces sour cream
12 ounces whole milk
3 ounces red food coloring
1 ounce pure vanilla extract

Vanilla Cream Cheese Frosting

1 pound, 8 ounces cream cheese, softened
6 ounces butter, softened
3 ounces sour cream
1 ounce pure vanilla extract
3 pounds confectioners' sugar

117

Cake

Preheat an oven to 330°F.

Mix the flour, cocoa powder, baking soda, and salt in a medium bowl. Set aside.

Beat the butter and sugar in a large bowl with an electric mixer on medium speed for 5 minutes or until light and fluffy. Beat in the eggs one at a time. Mix in the sour cream, milk, food coloring, and vanilla.

Gradually beat in the flour mixture on low speed until blended (do not over-beat).

Prepare 1 (12-inch), 1 (9-inch), and 1 (6-inch) pan with paper liners (grease the pans lightly so the paper liner will stick to the bottom and not move around).

Divide the batter in all three pans, making sure that the height of the batter is the same in all the pans.

Bake for 40 to 50 minutes or until a toothpick inserted into the cake comes out clean.

Cool in the pans on a wire rack for 15 minutes. Remove from the pans; cool completely. Refrigerate or freeze overnight.

Vanilla Cream Cheese Frosting

Beat the cream cheese, butter, sour cream, and vanilla extract in a large bowl until light and fluffy. Gradually beat in the confectioners' sugar until smooth.

Assembly

Remove the chilled cakes from the refrigerator or freezer. Split each cake twice with a serrated knife, creating three equally thick layers of each cake size.

Lay the bottom layer of each cake size flat on your work area. Top with a layer of cream cheese icing. Cover the layers of cream cheese icing with another layer of cake from the same-sized cake. Top with another layer of cream cheese icing. Cover each size of cake with the remaining layers of cake. Cool each cake separately in the refrigerator or freezer.

When chilled, remove the cakes, and ice each individually with cream cheese icing (you may choose to use buttercream for a lighter and smoother alternative). Chill, again.

When chilled, remove the cakes, and stack according to size to create a tiered cake (to prevent sliding or caving, you may insert wooden or plastic pegs [available in your baking supply store] for added support).

To decorate, use a decorating bag with a small plain tube filled with buttercream, and make buttercream scrolls in white all over the cake, starting from the top of the cake in a downward motion. In addition (or as an alternative), you may make or purchase gum-paste flowers, or use fresh-cut flowers for a special effect (see note below).

If you also choose to fill your cake with Cream Cheese Icing, double the icing recipe.

Gum paste flowers are also known as sugar, fondant, or royal icing flowers. You can shape and color them yourself to match the color scheme of your wedding, or you can purchase them at a bakery supply store. If you choose to use fresh edible flowers (such as roses, hibiscus, nasturtium, or pansies) on your wedding cake, be sure to use only certified organic, pesticide-free, non-toxic flowers. Before using, soak the flowers thoroughly, set on paper towels to completely dry, and insert into a flower holder so they won't touch the cake directly. It is best to use fresh flowers strictly as a garnish or decoration. They are beautiful cascading down a cake, but it's best to remove fresh flowers before serving the cake.

Italian Cassata Cream Cake

Serves 16

I could not believe it when I heard my nephew Billy's girlfriend Nora made him a cassata cake. That was just so romantic. It reminded me of my wedding cake. One of my first meals that I made for my then boyfriend—who turned out to be my wonderful husband Dennis—was a very fussy dinner: homemade appetizers through dessert. I still believe that the way to any person's heart is through their stomach. Yes, in some ways, I am old-fashioned. Taking the time to prepare something special for someone whom you care about is just another way of expressing love.

Story by Monica

Cake

4 eggs

⅔ cup sugar

1 cup all-purpose flour

½ cup unsalted butter, melted and cooled

1 tablespoon orange zest

Ricotta Filling

2 cups ricotta cheese

3 tablespoons sugar

2 teaspoons vanilla

1 cup heavy cream, whipped

1 cup semisweet chocolate mini-chips

Whipped Cream Icing

2 cups heavy cream

2 tablespoons confectioners' sugar

1 teaspoon vanilla

Cake

Preheat an oven to 350°F. Using a large bowl, beat together the eggs and sugar until thick (5 to 6 minutes). Fold in the flour, butter, and orange zest. Then pour into a greased and floured 8-inch-round baking pan. Bake for 40 minutes. Take out of the oven and cool for 5 minutes in the pan. Remove from the pan and cool completely on a wire rack.

Ricotta Filling

In a large bowl, beat the ricotta cheese, sugar, and vanilla using an electric mixer at medium speed for about 3 minutes. Fold in whipped heavy cream and mini-chocolate chips.

Whipped Cream Icing

Beat 2 cups of heavy cream on high until peaks form. Then beat in confectioners' sugar and vanilla.

Assembly

As the cake cools, make the ricotta filling. Cut the cooled cake in half horizontally. Then cut those two layers again horizontally. Place the first layer on a cake dish, and brush on ½ teaspoon of orange liquor or orange juice. Spread one-third of the ricotta filling over that, repeating this procedure with each layer, ending up with the cake as your top layer. Refrigerate for at least 6 hours or overnight. Following the refrigeration of the cake, make the whipped cream icing. Frost the sides and top with 1 cup of whipped cream icing, reserving 1 cup of icing for the second layer of icing. Refrigerate for 30 minutes; then ice the cake using the remaining 1 cup of icing (optional). You can also decorate the top of your iced cake with ½ cup of fresh raspberries from your garden, drained and dried mandarin orange slices, or shaved semisweet chocolate. Refrigerate until time to serve. Refrigerate any leftovers.

Vegetarian Mincemeat

Christine Gable, www.QuickMealHelp.com *(Lititz, PA)*
Serves 12

> This apple-based vegetarian mincemeat is a favorite holiday dessert. Kids can cut circles of pie crust to make tiny tarts, whether open-faced or topped with another circle. Spiced apple tarts are the perfect snack or dessert when wrapping gifts or entertaining friends during the holiday season. Another added bonus is the simmering filling makes the house smell fabulous.

6 medium apples, peeled and sliced
1 cup raisins
¼ cup light olive oil
1 tablespoon lemon zest
1 tablespoon lemon juice
¼ teaspoon ground allspice
½ teaspoon ground cinnamon
⅛ teaspoon ground cloves
¼ teaspoon salt
1 cup water
1 tablespoon cornstarch
⅓ cup water
1 tablespoon orange liqueur (such as Grand Marnier®)
2 prepared pie crusts, store-bought or homemade (see page 191)
Confectioners' sugar, to garnish (optional)

To make the filling: Place the first 10 ingredients in a medium saucepan and bring to a boil. Lower the heat and simmer, covered, for 30 minutes. Stir occasionally during cooking. Remove the lid, and simmer for another 30 minutes or until thick.

Dissolve the cornstarch in the water. While stirring, slowly add the cornstarch-water mixture to the cooked filling until thickened and translucent. Remove from the heat, and stir in the orange liqueur. Let cool (will keep in a refrigerator for 2 to 3 weeks).

For open-faced tarts, top the pie crust rounds (about 2 inches in diameter) with 1 tablespoon of filling, and bake at 375°F for 15 minutes. For closed tarts, top the filling with the second piece of crust, and then bake. Remove from oven, let cool briefly, and sprinkle with confectioners' sugar (optional).

Vanilla Cupcakes

Serves 24

These cupcakes were my son's favorite for birthday parties at school. My neighbor gave me this simple recipe from her cookbook when she realized that I had never baked cupcakes before. Thank goodness for her: she was always there when I needed her after my husband had died. I often had to go over and borrow some of the ingredients, as well.

Cupcakes

1 cup sugar

2 cups flour

½ teaspoon salt

3 teaspoons baking powder

¼ cup butter, melted

1 cup light cream

1 egg, beaten

1½ teaspoons vanilla

Vanilla Icing

1 teaspoon butter

4 tablespoons hot milk

3 cups confectioners' sugar

2 teaspoons vanilla

Cupcakes

Preheat an oven to 375°F. Sift together the dry ingredients. Mix the butter, cream, egg, and vanilla together. Combine both mixtures. Bake for 20 minutes in medium cupcake tins lined with decorative paper liners. Cool on a wire rack, and ice.

Vanilla Icing

Add the butter to the milk, slowly add the sugar until smooth, and then mix in the vanilla. Spread on the cupcakes. Refrigerate any leftover icing for future use within 1 week.

Using food coloring, you can change the color of this icing. You can also vary the color using sprinkles or colored sugar.

Greek Butter Cookies (Kourambiedes)

Chef Stavros Kokkosis "Steve," Aegean Café *(Sayville, NY)*
Yields 5 dozen cookies

4-5 cups sifted flour
1 teaspoon baking powder
2 cups butter
½ cup sugar
2 egg yolks
1 tablespoon ouzo
1 teaspoon vanilla
1 cup sliced and toasted almonds
1 tablespoon flower or rose water
1½ pounds confectioners' sugar

Preheat an oven to 300°F. Set aside 1 cup of the flour. Mix the baking powder into the remaining flour. Cream the butter in a bowl until very light, then add to it the sugar and eggs, beating continuously until thoroughly blended. Add the ouzo, vanilla, and sliced almonds, mixing well. Slowly add 2 to 3 cups of the dry ingredients, knead well, and then knead in the rest a little at a time.

Because the size of the eggs—as well as the weather—can affect the consistency of the dough, check it as follows to be sure that it is right for handling: using the palms of your hands, roll a small piece of dough into a fat cord about as thick as your finger, and shape it into an "S." If the curves of the "S" show little cracks, then the dough has enough flour. If not (or if the dough is too soft to handle), add a little more flour (from the reserved cup), kneading it in well. After you have made these cookies a few times, you will acquire the "feel" of the dough.

When the dough has the proper texture, pinch off pieces, roll them as above, and shape into traditional "S" shapes, circles, or crescents. Place on a buttered baking sheet, and bake for 15 to 20 minutes.

As soon as you remove the cookies from the oven, sprinkle them with the flower water and dust thickly with confectioners' sugar. Serve in individual paper cups or cupcake liners for easier handling.

Cream Cheese Butter Cookies

Marlisa Brown, M.S., R.D., C.D.E. *(Bay Shore, NY)*
Recipe first published in *Gluten-Free, Hassle-Free: A Simple, Sane, Dietician-Approved Program for Eating Your Way Back to Health*

> These cookies are simple to make, and are the ultimate buttery cookie to dip into coffee. These cookies have been adapted from my mother-in-law Helen's famous cream cheese cookies.

2 sticks (1 cup) unsalted butter or margarine
1 (3 oz.) package cream cheese, softened
1 cup granulated sugar
1 egg yolk
1 teaspoon vanilla extract
3½ cups all-purpose Gluten-Free Flour (see next page)
1 teaspoon salt
2 teaspoon xanthan gum
¼ cup powdered sugar

Preheat an oven to 350°F. In a large bowl, cream together the butter and cream cheese. Add sugar, and blend until smooth. Add egg yolk and vanilla to the butter mixture, and mix to combine. In a small bowl, combine the gluten-free flour, salt, and xanthan gum. Combine the wet and dry ingredients until a nice dough forms. Shape the cookies into small balls, and make a thumb print in the center. Place the cookies on a cookie sheet and bake for 10 to 12 minutes until they are light gold in color. Remove from the cookie sheet and place on aluminum foil or a rack to cool. Sprinkle with powdered sugar, and store in an airtight container until ready to use.

Gluten-Free Flour

Makes 4½ cups

1½ cups sorghum flour
1½ cups potato starch or corn starch
1 cup tapioca flour
½ cup chickpea flour, corn flour, almond flour, or hazelnut flour

Mix together all the ingredients and store any leftover for future use in an airtight container.

Baklava

Chef Stavros Kokkosis, "Steve," Aegean Café (*Sayville, NY*)
Serves 12

> I can never leave Chef Steve's restaurant without a piece of baklava: a tender, sweet Greek confection dripping with honey. He has been kind enough to share his recipe for this all-time favorite so you can try it at home.
>
> *Story by Monica*

4 cups chopped walnuts
½ cup sugar
1 tablespoon cinnamon
1½ pounds phyllo (13 sheets)
1¼ cups butter, melted

Syrup
4 cups sugar
3 cups water
½ cup honey
1 piece cinnamon stick
4-5 cloves

Preheat an oven to 250°F. Mix together the walnuts, sugar, and cinnamon. Select a pan the size of the phyllo sheets, and brush well with melted butter. Use four sheets of phyllo for the bottom layer, brushing each one with butter before adding the next layer. Top with a sheet of unbuttered phyllo, and sprinkle a handful of the walnuts on it. Cover with a sheet of buttered phyllo, and then, again, with an unbuttered one. Sprinkle the last sheet with a handful of walnuts. Continue in this manner until all of the ingredients are used, reserving five phyllo sheets for the top layer. Brush the top sheet with the remaining butter. Trim the edges, if necessary. Score the baklava into diamond-shaped pieces without cutting through the bottom layers. Wet your fingers and shake them over the baklava to sprinkle the top with water. Bake for about 1 hour. Remove from the oven and cool.

Syrup

Put the sugar and water in a large pot, and bring to a boil. Boil for 5 minutes. Add the honey, cinnamon, and cloves, and boil for another 5 minutes. Pour this hot syrup onto the cold baklava. Cool; then cut through the bottom layer and serve (always pour hot over cold to reduce sogginess). The baklava should be crisp, yet moist.

Christmas Rum Cakes

Nora Rooney *(Raleigh, NC)*
Serves 8-10

> This recipe has been shared with me by my godmother, who lives in Grand Rapids, Michigan. I have never made these rum cakes myself, but my godmother has made them for me countless times, and they are fantastic. She makes them as mini-Bundt cakes, and wraps them in plastic wrap to give as Christmas presents. They are also great when served with French vanilla ice cream.

1 box yellow cake mix with pudding
4 eggs
½ cup vegetable oil
¼ cup water
¼ cup dark rum
Whole pecans, to garnish
Maraschino cherries, halved, to garnish

Topping
1 stick butter
½ cup sugar
½ cup dark rum

Preheat an oven to 350°F. Mix together the cake mix, eggs, oil, water, and rum. Beat on a medium setting for 2 minutes (the batter will be very thick). Copiously spray a Bundt cake pan with baking spray, and arrange the whole pecans and halved maraschino cherries upside-down in the bottom of the pan. Fill the pan with the batter, and bake as instructed on the cake mix box.

Topping

Bring the butter, sugar, and rum to a boil in a small saucepan.

Just after removing the cake from the oven and while still in the pan, poke the cake with a knife or fork, and pour the boiling topping over the cake. Let the cake sit for 20 minutes at room temperature on a cooling rack before removing the cake from the Bundt pan.

This cake can be made ahead and frozen until ready to use. You can also adapt this recipe to use mini-Bundt pans.

Triple Chocolate Brownies

Christopher Holt, Executive Chef, The George Martin Group
(Rockville Centre, NY)
Serves 6

½ cup semi-sweet chocolate chips
1 stick butter
2 large eggs
1 cup sugar
⅓ cup all-purpose flour
½ teaspoon vanilla extract
⅛ cup bittersweet chocolate chips
⅛ cup white chocolate chips

Melt semi-sweet chocolate and butter in the microwave for about 90 seconds. Stir to combine and set aside.

Beat eggs and sugar for about one minute, until fluffy. Mix in chocolate/butter mixture.

Add flour and vanilla extract. Mix to combine.

Pour batter into a buttered 8- x 8-inch baking pan. Sprinkle top with bittersweet and white chocolate chips. Gently press into the batter.

Bake at 325°F for about 40 minutes. Cool one hour before cutting.

Crustless Cranberry Pie

Maria Zenk, Zenk's Prairie Vine Farm *(Danube, MN)*

1 cup all-purpose flour
1 cup white sugar
¼ teaspoon salt
2 cups cranberries (or other fruits or berries, or chopped rhubarb)
½ cup chopped walnuts or pecans
½ cup butter, melted
2 eggs, beaten
1 teaspoon almond extract, vanilla extract, or orange zest
Brown sugar, to taste

Preheat an oven to 350°F. Grease a 9-inch pie pan or an 8- x 8-inch pan.

Combine the flour, sugar, and salt. Stir in the cranberries and walnuts, tossing to coat. Stir in the butter, beaten eggs, and almond extract (if using frozen cranberries, the mixture will be very thick). Spread the batter into the prepared pan. Sprinkle brown sugar over the top. Bake for 40 minutes or until a toothpick inserted near the center comes out clean. Serve warm with whipped cream (see page 120) or ice cream.

Hawaiian Carrot Cake

Serves 12-16

> This moist carrot cake is one of my mom's favorite choices for her birthday cakes. I make several different kinds of carrot cake, but adding the pineapple is a unique surprise with every bite, and makes for a very moist cake.
>
> *Story by Monica*

Cake

4 eggs

1 cup white sugar

1 cup light brown sugar

1 cup extra-virgin olive oil

2 cups all-purpose flour

3 tablespoons cinnamon

¾ teaspoon baking soda

½ teaspoon baking powder

¼ teaspoon salt

⅛ teaspoon nutmeg

⅛ teaspoon cloves

2 cups carrots, washed, dried, peeled, and grated

⅛ cup crushed pineapple

Frosting

½ cup butter, softened

3 ounces cream cheese, softened

2 teaspoons vanilla extract

4 cups confectioners' sugar

3-4 tablespoons warm milk

1 cup chopped walnuts

Cake

Preheat an oven to 350°F. Grease two 9-inch baking pans. Using a large mixing bowl, combine the eggs, sugars, and oil. Combine the flour, cinnamon, baking soda, baking powder, salt, nutmeg, and cloves. Mix with the egg mixture. Beat for 1 minute. Stir in the carrots and pineapple. Pour the mixture evenly into the baking pans, and bake for 35 to 40 minutes or until a skewer inserted comes out clean. Cool in the pans on a wire rack for 10 minutes, then turn out and cool completely on the rack.

Frosting

Cream the butter and cream cheese. Mix in the vanilla, and then beat in confectioners' sugar, ⅛ cup at a time. Add milk until smooth enough to spread. Mix in the walnuts. Cut the cake into two layers horizontally. First, spread over the bottom layer of the cake. Place the top layer of the cake, and spread the icing over the top and sides of cake. Refrigerate until ready to serve.

Gluten-Free Cheesecake Bars

Marlisa Brown, M.S., R.D., C.D.E. *(Bay Shore, NY)*
Recipe first published in *Gluten-Free, Hassle-Free: A Simple, Sane, Dietician-Approved Program for Eating Your Way Back to Health*
Serves 36 (1 bar each)

> These delicious bars are like mini-cheesecakes—perfect for an afternoon treat.

¾ cup crushed gluten-free graham crackers
½ cup Gluten-Free Flour (see page 129)
½ cup chopped walnuts
¼ cup sugar
½ cup butter, melted
1 (8 oz.) package cream cheese
⅓ cup sugar
1 egg
1 tablespoon lemon juice
½ teaspoon grated lemon peel

Preheat an oven to 350°F. Stir together the graham crackers, flour, walnuts, and ¼ cup of sugar, reserving 2 tablespoons of the graham cracker crumbs. Add melted butter, and combine. Press into a 9- x 9-inch square nonstick baking pan. Bake for 12 minutes. Cream together the cream cheese and ⅓ cup of sugar. Add egg, lemon juice, and lemon peel, mixing well. Pour over the baked layer, and sprinkle with the remaining graham cracker crumbs. Bake for an additional 20 to 25 minutes. Cool, and cut into bars.

Neapolitan Cookies

Suzanne Link *(Sayville, NY)*
Makes 3 dozen

> These light crispy cookies are a favorite in our house. I first
> made them at Christmas when my kids were very young. My
> kids are now in college, but every Christmas, they still ask for
> them. They are the first ones on the cookie platter to disappear.

1 cup butter, softened
1½ cups white sugar
1 egg
1 teaspoon vanilla extract
2½ cups all-purpose flour
1½ teaspoons baking powder
½ teaspoon salt
½ teaspoon almond extract
5 drops red food coloring
1 (1 oz.) square unsweetened chocolate, melted
½ cup chopped walnuts

In a medium bowl, cream together the butter and sugar. Stir in the
egg and vanilla. Combine the flour, baking powder, and salt; stir into
a creamed mixture. Divide the dough equally into three small bowls.
Add almond extract and red food coloring to one bowl; stir until thoroughly mixed. Mix the melted and cooled chocolate into the second
bowl, and, lastly, add walnuts into the third bowl.

Line a 9- x 5-inch loaf pan with waxed paper, and spread the almond
dough (pink mixture) into the pan. Layer with the walnut dough and
top with the chocolate dough. Cover with waxed paper and refrigerate
until firm (about 4 hours).

Preheat an oven to 350°F. Turn out the chilled dough by inverting
the pan; peel off the waxed paper. With a sharp knife, cut the dough
lengthwise in half and then slice each half into ¼-inch slices. Place
the slices 1-inch apart on a cookie sheet. Bake for 10 to 12 minutes or
until lightly browned. Cool on wire racks.

Fantastic Carrot Cake

Nora Rooney *(Raleigh, NC)*
Serves 12-14

> This carrot cake is a recipe that I received about fourteen years ago from my friend Christine. The frosting is so good, and I dare say that I have made it even better than the original recipe by adding Cointreau® to the frosting. It is one of the only cakes with which I really love eating the frosting in large quantities.

Cake

2 cups all-purpose flour
2 teaspoons baking soda
2 teaspoons cinnamon
1 teaspoon salt
½ teaspoon nutmeg
Pinch cloves
4 large eggs
1 cup granulated sugar
¾ cup packed brown sugar
1 teaspoon vanilla extract
1 cup vegetable oil
3 cups (about 1 pound) shredded carrots
1 cup nuts, chopped

Cream Cheese Icing

1 (8 oz.) package cream cheese, softened
¼ cup butter
1 teaspoon vanilla extract
Grated orange peel from half of 1 large orange
1 tablespoon Cointreau®
3 cups confectioners' sugar

Cake

Preheat an oven to 350°F. Butter two 8-inch square or 9-inch round cake pans. Line the bottoms with waxed paper. Butter and flour the paper; tap to remove any excess flour.

Combine the flour, baking soda, cinnamon, salt, nutmeg, and cloves in a small bowl. Combine the eggs, granulated sugar, brown sugar, and vanilla in a large mixing bowl, and beat at medium speed until smooth. With the mixer at low speed, gradually add oil in a thin, steady stream until blended. Add dry ingredients and beat just until blended. Fold in the carrots and nuts with a rubber spatula. Spoon into prepared pans.

Bake for 40 to 45 minutes or until a toothpick inserted in the center comes out clean. Cool in the pans on a wire rack for 10 minutes. Invert the cakes onto the racks. Carefully peel off the waxed paper, then cool completely right-side up. This cake can be made ahead and saved for later use. Simply wrap well and store at room temperature up to 24 hours. Refrigerate for 24 hours before serving for optimal taste.

Cream Cheese Icing

Combine the cream cheese, butter, vanilla, and orange peel in a large mixing bowl. Add Cointreau®. Beat at medium-high speed until light and fluffy, scraping the bowl occasionally. Beat in confectioners' sugar to a spreading consistency.

Place one layer of cake, which has been cut horizontally on a cake plate, and spread with one-third of icing. Top with a second layer. Spread the top and sides with the remaining icing. Press the chopped walnuts along the sides of the cake (optional).

For a large show-stopping cake, double the recipe and bake the doubled recipe in two 8-inch-square or 9-inch-round cake pans for about 80 minutes or until a toothpick in the center comes out clean.

After cooling the cakes as detailed above, level the top of the cakes by slicing the rounded top off the cakes with a knife or cake leveler. Cut each of the two cakes into two separate layers of equal thickness.

Place one layer on the cake plate, cut-side up, and cover with frosting. Add other layers and repeat, frosting each layer with a consistently thick layer of frosting. Add the last layer, cut-side down, and frost the outside of the cake.

Make additional frosting for thicker frosting layers or for decorating by adding a few drops of food coloring.

Jeannine's Ricotta Cookies

Jeannine Rocco *(Bellport, NY)*
Makes 3-4 dozen

> This is an old Italian recipe that I love to share with friends and family.

Cookies

2 cups sugar
1 cup soft butter
1 (15 oz.) container ricotta
2 teaspoons vanilla
2 large eggs
4 cups flour
2 tablespoons baking powder
1 teaspoon salt

Icing

1½ cups confectioners' sugar
3 tablespoons milk
1 jar white or colored sprinkles

Cookies

Mix the sugar and butter until light and fluffy. Add ricotta, vanilla, and eggs. Then add flour, baking powder, and salt. Refrigerate the dough for 2 hours.

Preheat an oven to 350°F.

Drop the small-sized balls a onto cookie sheet 2-inches apart. Put in the oven and back for 12 to 15 minutes or until the cookies are very lightly browned. Let the cookies cool.

Icing

Mix together all the ingredients until thick (add more confectioners' sugar, if needed). Use a spoon to drip the icing on the top of each cookie, then garnishing with nonpareil sprinkles while the icing is still wet.

Double Chocolate Chip Cookies

Marlisa Brown, M.S., R.D., C.D.E. *(Bay Shore, NY)*
Recipe first published in *Gluten-Free, Hassle-Free: A Simple, Sane, Dietician-Approved Program for Eating Your Way Back to Health*
Makes 4 dozen

> This is the ultimate chocolate chip cookie—no one would ever know that they are gluten-free.

2¼ cups Gluten-Free Flour (see page 129)
½ cup brown rice flour
2 teaspoons gluten-free baking soda
1 teaspoon gluten-free baking powder
1 teaspoon salt
2 teaspoons xanthan gum
2 sticks butter
2 eggs, slightly beaten
1 teaspoon vanilla extract
¾ cup white sugar
¾ cup brown sugar
1 (12 oz.) bag gluten-free semisweet chocolate chips
1 (6 oz.) bag gluten-free semisweet chocolate chunks

Preheat an oven to 350°F. Combine all the dry ingredients (except the sugars and chips). Cream the butter, then add sugar and beat until well combined. Add eggs and vanilla extract to the butter mixture, and mix well. Mix the flour mixture into the creamed mixture (if too wet, add a little extra flour blend or brown rice flour). The dough should be moist, but hold together well. Add ¾ of the chips, reserving the rest of the chips and chocolate chunks for topping. Use a tablespoon scoop to place the cookies on the baking sheet (spray the scoop with cooking spray to keep the dough from sticking). Spoon three cookies across on each row on the baking sheet, because they may spread out onto each other. Top the cookies with reserved chocolate chips and chunks, pushing into each cookie a little. Bake the cookies until they are just starting to brown, but are still a little light in the middle (approximately 7 to 10 minutes). Remove from the oven and let sit for about 1 to 2 minutes. Remove from the baking sheet and cool on aluminum foil or a rack.

Pumpkin Crunch

Joyce Barber, Breezy Acres Bed and Breakfast *(Hobart, NY)*
Serves 15

> This is a great semi-homemade recipe that will save you time
> while yielding excellent results. I have selected this for our Bed
> and Breakfast because we grow our own pumpkins. Enjoy!

2 cups pumpkin puree
1 (12 oz.) can evaporated milk
3 large eggs
1½ cups sugar
1 teaspoon cinnamon
½ teaspoon salt
1 box yellow cake mix
1 cup chopped pecans
1 cup butter, melted

Preheat an oven to 350°F. Grease the bottom of a 13- x 9-inch pan.
Combine the first six ingredients and pour into the prepared pan.
Sprinkle with the cake mix. Top with the chopped pecans, and
drizzle with butter. Do not stir. Bake for 50 to 55 minutes or until
tests done.

Crescent Pastry

Suzanne Link *(Sayville, NY)*
Makes 1 dozen

> This recipe was handed down to my mother from my Italian grandmother. I remember making these cookie-like flaky pastries as a kid with my mother. We would spread the dough out on the table and work together. These were a family favorite among my siblings. We called them "Nanny's crescent cookies."

Dough
2 cups sifted flour
½ pound butter or margarine
¾ cup sour cream
1 egg yolk

Filling
¾ cup chopped walnuts
1 teaspoon cinnamon
¾ cup sugar

Dough

Measure the flour and butter into a bowl. Cut the butter into the flour with your fingers, and then add sour cream and egg yolk. Divide the dough and roll into four balls. Cover in plastic wrap, and refrigerate or freeze for later use.

Filling

Preheat an oven to 350°F. Mix together all the ingredients. Roll out one ball of dough at a time. Cut into triangles and sprinkle with the filling mixture. Roll each triangle with filling from wide end to tip. Place on a cookie sheet and bend into a semicircular shape. Bake for 20 to 30 minutes.

Ricotta Cookies

Joyce Barber, Breezy Acres Bed and Breakfast *(Hobart, NY)*
Makes 5 dozen

> These cookies are great for all occasions. After frosting, simply
> shake on colored sugars or sprinkles.

Cookies

4 cups flour
1 teaspoon baking soda
1 teaspoon salt
3 teaspoons baking powder
½ pound butter, softened
1 pound ricotta cheese
2 eggs
2 cups sugar
2 teaspoons vanilla

Icing

2 cups confectioners' sugar
Few drops almond flavoring
Milk, as needed to reach desired consistency

Cookies

Preheat an oven to 350°F. Combine the flour, baking soda, salt, and
baking powder. In a large bowl, cream the butter, ricotta, eggs, sugar,
and vanilla. Stir in the dry ingredients.

Drop by heaping tablespoonfuls on a greased cookie sheet. Bake for
12 to 15 minutes. Ice when cooled.

Icing

Combine all the ingredients to make a spreadable consistency.

Apple Pie

Mary Carlin *(East Meadow, NY)*
Serves 8

> My mother-in-law taught me to bake this family favorite. I have since taught many friends to bake it in my own kitchen to bring to family gatherings during the holidays. Use a deep dish to bake this traditional American apple pie.

7 apples, green Cortland, Rome, or McIntosh
1 (9-inch) pie crust (see page 191)
¾ cups sugar
1½-2 teaspoons cinnamon
1 tablespoon flour
4 tablespoons butter
1 egg white, used as wash

Preheat an oven to 425°F. Slice the apples, and put them evenly into a 9-inch pie plate lined with crust. Mix the sugar, cinnamon, and flour together, and then sprinkle over apples. Put dots of butter all over the top of the apples. Add pastry top. Prick open in the center to vent. With a pastry brush dipped into milk or egg white, coat the surface to protect from burning. Bake for 15 minutes, but then reduce the heat to 325°F and bake for another 30 to 40 minutes or until brown.

Pineapple Upside-Down Cake

Serves 8

⅓ cup butter
½ cup brown sugar
8 slices fresh, ripe pineapple, cut into rings with holes in the center
(see note)
8 maraschino cherries
½-1 cup unsalted pecans
2 eggs
⅔ cup sugar
6 tablespoons pineapple juice
1 teaspoon vanilla
1 cup flour
⅓ cup baking powder
½ teaspoon salt

Preheat an oven to 350°F. Melt the butter in a microwave for about 40 seconds, and pour into a 12-inch round baking dish. Sprinkle brown sugar into the butter, and mix together, spreading over the entire bottom of the dish. Place the pineapple rings on top of the mixture, and place a cherry into the hole of each pineapple ring. In between each pineapple, place pecans to fill in all the spaces. Beat the eggs, gradually add sugar, and beat, again. Add pineapple juice and vanilla. Sift the flour, baking powder, and salt, beat, and then pour over the fruit. Bake for 45 minutes or until a skewer comes out clean. Immediately turn onto a serving plate. Serve with whipped cream (see page 120) beaten with a bit of dark rum, sugar, and vanilla.

Instead of using cherries, soak banana slices in dark rum, and place in the center of each pineapple ring. You can also try using salted pecans in place of unsalted.

Cutting your pineapple for this recipe may seem daunting, but it really isn't. To cut your fresh pineapple, first twist off the leaves on top. Hold the leaves with a dishtowel so as not to cut your fingers (this should be easy if the pineapple is nice and ripe). Cut the top and bottom of the pineapple using a large knife so they are both flat and easier to work with. Place on a flat surface and begin cutting lengthwise around the whole pineapple (about ½ inch deep). Continue around the whole pineapple, overlapping each cut slightly (any remaining divots in the flesh can be removed with a potato peeler). Cut into slices using a small knife, and cut out the rough core of each individual slice to create a circle in the middle of each slice. Pop out the center, and it is ready to use. Pour any accumulated juice on the cutting board into your batter.

To cut the pineapple into chunks, follow the directions above, but rather than cutting into circles after peeling, cut into 4 slices lengthwise. Tip the pineapple slightly onto the side of each quarter, and cut out the center core in one cut. Then slice each quarter into your desired thickness, and cube. Refrigerate any unused portions.

Tea Time Tessies

Jeannine Rocco *(Bellport, NY)*
Makes 1 dozen

> My great-grandma Lillian made these cookies. They are delicious.

Tart Shells

1 cup flour
¼ pound butter
3 ounces cream cheese, softened

Filling

2 tablespoons butter
1 cup packed brown sugar
1 teaspoon vanilla
1 egg
1 cup pecans, finely chopped
⅛-¼ cup confectioners' sugar, for dusting

Tart Shells

Preheat an oven to 375°F. Mix the flour, butter, and cream cheese until a dough forms. Make 1-inch balls, and place in a mini-muffin pan, pressing the dough down to configure the shape (the dough should be thin).

Filling

Place the butter, brown sugar, and vanilla in a pan. Heat until melted, then add egg and stir well. Add the pecans, and mix thoroughly.

Place the filling into the tart shells to the rim. Bake for 20 minutes. Place on a plate and let cool. Once cooled, sprinkle confectioners' sugar on top.

Mom's Christmas Cookies

Jeannine Rocco *(Bellport, NY)*
Makes 2 dozen

> This recipe has been passed down from my husband's Grandma
> Knapp to his mother. Every Christmas, my husband Mike would
> help his mom make Grandma's Christmas cookies. His mother
> has now passed, but we still make these Christmas cookies
> together each year and reminisce.

1 cup Crisco®
1 cup sugar
1 teaspoon vanilla
1 egg
2 cups flour
1 teaspoon baking powder
½ teaspoon salt

Mix together the Crisco® and sugar until creamy. Add vanilla and
egg, and then flour, baking powder, and salt. Shape into a roll ½-inch
in diameter. Wrap in waxed paper and refrigerate for 1 to 2 hours. Cut
the dough into thin slices and place on a cookie sheet. Bake at 325°F
for 12 to 15 minutes.

Before baking, you can also add any flavor of jam (see page 27) you
like or sprinkles on top of the cookies.

Chocolate Chip Drops

Jeannine Rocco (*Bellport, NY*)
Makes 2 dozen

> This recipe was given to me by a wonderful client many years ago.

2 sticks butter, softened
½ cup sifted powdered sugar
1 teaspoon vanilla
2 cups all-purpose flour
⅔ cup finely chopped nuts
1 (12 oz.) package semisweet chocolate chips

Preheat an oven to 350°F. Beat the butter and powdered sugar until creamy, then add vanilla. Gradually add flour and nuts. Add 1 1/2 cups of chocolate chips. Roll into 1-inch balls onto an ungreased baking pan. Bake for 10 to 12 minutes. Remove the cookies and cool on a rack. Melt the remaining chocolate and drizzle onto each cookie.

Creamy Chocolate Mint Brownies

Nora Rooney *(Raleigh, NC)*
Yields 1 dozen

1 cup sugar
½ cup unsalted butter, softened
1 cup all-purpose flour
2 cups chocolate syrup
4 large eggs, beaten
½ teaspoon salt
1 teaspoon vanilla extract

Mint Topping

2½ cups confectioners' sugar
½ cup unsalted butter, melted
3 tablespoons peppermint extract

Chocolate Topping

1 cup semisweet chocolate chips
6 tablespoons unsalted butter

Preheat an oven to 325°F. Butter a 9-by-13-inch pan.
Cream together the sugar and softened butter. Stir in the flour, and mix well. Add the chocolate syrup, eggs, salt, and vanilla, and mix everything well. Pour the batter into the pan, baking for 25 minutes. Let cool.

Mint Topping

Mix the confectioners' sugar, melted butter, and peppermint extract until smooth. Taste to see if you need more peppermint extract. Let cool slightly, and spread over the cooled brownies.

Chocolate Topping

Melt the chocolate chips in the butter, and pour over the mint topping. Let the brownies and mint toppings cool completely (you can even put them in the refrigerator).

Grammy's Cupcakes

Rosemarie McGraw *(Bethlehem, PA)*
Makes 48 cupcakes

No trip to or from our in-laws in Pennsylvania is ever complete without Grammy's Cupcakes. When my kids were little, they stood on a chair at her counter with a wooden spoon way too big for their little hands, helping Grammy make these tasty treats. In between each stir was the sly handful of chocolate chips that were popped into the mouths of babes—and on-looking grown-ups, as well. Cupcakes may be the newest dessert on the market today, but Grammy's Cupcakes have been all the rage in our family since the kids could say "yummy!"

Story by Patty McGraw

Cupcakes
4½ cups flour
3 cups sugar
¾ cup cocoa
3 teaspoons white vinegar
3 teaspoons vanilla
1½ teaspoons salt
3 cups cold water
1½ cups oil

Filling
24 ounces cream cheese, softened
1 cup sugar
3 eggs
24 ounces chocolate chips (add after other three ingredients have been combined)

Cupcakes

Mix all the ingredients in a large bowl. Fill the cupcake trays slightly more than halfway.

Filling

Preheat an oven to 350°F. Mix all the ingredients (except the chocolate chips), and add a tablespoon of filling into each cupcake. Top each with chocolate chips, and bake for 20 minutes.

▌ Grammy's Cupcakes freeze beautifully. When making a batch for
▌ your next special occasion, go ahead and make some extra for a
▌ great surprise treat anytime.

Cake Pops

Yield 3-4 dozen

These are just a mouthful of pure pleasure. Cake Pops are great for parties and baby showers, and are also nice either as a thoughtful individually wrapped treat for your co-workers or a dozen wrapped up in a gift box to give at Christmas.

Story by Monica

1 recipe white cake mix (page 187) or 1 (14¼-ounce) box cake mix
¾ cup frosting (see page 188)

Chocolate Dip
1 (24 oz.) package chocolate candy coating

Bake the cake according to the recipe or instructions on the box. Cool enough to work with, and crumble into a large bowl. Stir in ½ cup of frosting. Mix until completely combined (like the consistency of a truffle). Add more frosting, if necessary, to get the right consistency, but don't let it get mushy. Roll into 1-inch balls. Line up on a cookie sheet and cover with plastic wrap. Refrigerate overnight. Refrigerate any unused frosting for future use for up to 1 week.

Chocolate Dip

Melt the chocolate candy coating according to the package instructions. Dip the tip of the lollipop stick into the melted candy coating, and insert into the bottom of the cake ball almost halfway in. Holding by the stick, gently insert the cake pop into the melted candy coating, rotating it until it is completely covered. Carefully tap off any excess chocolate, and rotate to fully coat. At this point, sprinkle on sprinkles or colored sugar before the dipped lollipop has a chance to set. Stick each lollipop into a Styrofoam™ board covered in plastic wrap until thoroughly set. Once set, wrap each lollipop individually in clear cellophane bags, and tie with ribbon.

Supply List

(These items can be purchased at your local craft store.)

1 Styrofoam™ board

Plastic wrap, to cover board

Small 3 to 4-inch cellophane treat bags

1 roll curling ribbon

4 dozen lollipop sticks

Dark Chocolate Brownies

Maria Zenk, Zenk's Prairie Vine Farm *(Danube, MN)*
Makes 1 dozen

1⅔ cups dark chocolate morsels, divided
1 cup granulated sugar
⅓ cup butter, cut into pieces
2 tablespoons water
2 large eggs
1 teaspoon vanilla extract
¾ cup all-purpose flour
¼ teaspoon salt
½ cup chopped walnuts or pecans (optional)

Preheat an oven to 325°F. Grease an 8-inch-square baking pan. Set aside ⅓ cup of morsels.

Heat 1⅓ cups of morsels, sugar, butter, and water in a small saucepan over low heat, stirring constantly until the chocolate and butter are melted. Pour into a medium bowl. Stir in the eggs one at a time with a wire whisk until blended. Stir in the vanilla extract. Add flour and salt; stir well. Then stir in the remaining ⅓ cup of morsels and nuts. Pour into the prepared baking pan. Bake for 38 to 40 minutes or until a toothpick inserted in the center comes out slightly sticky. Cool in the pan on a wire rack. Cut into bars.

Old-Fashioned Molasses Cookies

Christine Gable *(Published on Quick Meal Help)*
Serves 12

> This truly is an old-fashioned molasses cookie recipe. Be sure to mix these by hand, because overbeating any of the ingredients can cause the cookies to become flat when baked. I also suggest using the green label Brer Rabbit® molasses—that's the ticket to baking the best molasses cookies.
>
> This recipe is from my grandmother Kathryn Plowfield. Since this is a large recipe, it may be best to make only half a batch (which makes about three dozen cookies). If you prefer a larger cookie, you can increase the size of the scooped batter on the cookie sheet and extend the baking time.

½ cup vegetable shortening
½ cup butter or margarine
2 cups brown sugar, packed
2 eggs
1 cup Brer Rabbit® molasses
5 cups flour, slightly rounded
4 teaspoons baking soda
1 cup buttermilk

Preheat an oven to 375°F. In a large bowl with a wooden spoon, mix the shortening, butter, and brown sugar until creamy. Add eggs and molasses, and stir until evenly mixed. In a separate bowl, stir together the flour and baking soda (or dry-whisk to mix it evenly). Add the dry ingredients to the creamed sugar mixture alternately with the buttermilk. Stir until the soft batter forms (just until all the flour is incorporated). Spoon the dough into 1-inch scoops onto a cookie sheet or baking stone. Bake for 15 minutes or until puffy and done in the middle. Remove from the oven, and allow to cool on the sheet for 1 minute before removing with a spatula to cool completely. Serve warm or cool.

Dominican Brownies

Elinor Cabrera *(Santo Domingo, Dominican Republic)*

> This is a very classic brownie recipe. I don't have an interesting
> story behind it: only that I love brownies, and started baking
> them since I was nine years old, always using Dominican cocoa
> powder for a more original flavor. You can purchase Dominican
> chocolate (also known as "Cocoa Sobrino" or "Hermanos Cortes")
> at Dominican groceries.

1 stick butter
½ cup Dominican cocoa powder (or Dominican semisweet chocolate
bars, shredded)
2 whole eggs
1 cup white sugar (or Dominican raw sugar)
1 cup flour
1 teaspoon baking powder
1 teaspoon vanilla extract

Preheat an oven to 350°F. In a pan, melt the butter, and mix in the
cocoa until no clumps show. In a bowl, beat the eggs, add sugar,
and mix well. Add the butter and cocoa mixture to the eggs and
sugar, and stir well. Slowly add the flour and baking powder with a
sifter, and finally add the vanilla extract. Pour the brownie mixture
in a baking pan greased with butter. Bake for 20 minutes or until a
toothpick inserted in the center comes out clean. For a more fudge-
like consistency, take out of the oven when it is still a little wet.

For a cake-like brownie, add more cocoa and sugar. For a fudgy
brownie, use two sticks of butter instead of one. You can also try
adding walnuts before baking.

Rockin' Vegan Oatmeal Nut Cookies

Liz Finnegan *(Islip, NY)*
Serves 12

2 cups quick-cooking oats
1 cup all-purpose flour
1 cup whole-wheat flour
1 teaspoon baking soda
½ teaspoon baking powder
½ teaspoon salt
⅔ cup canola oil
⅔ cup sugar
¾ cup dark brown sugar, firmly packed
½ cup non-dairy milk
1½ teaspoons vanilla extract
1 cup shredded coconut
1 cup semisweet chocolate chips
1 cup pecans, toasted and chopped

Preheat an oven to 350°F. Line two baking pans with parchment paper. In a medium-sized bowl, stir together the oats, flour, baking soda, baking powder, and salt. In a large bowl, beat the oil, sugar, brown sugar, non-dairy milk, and vanilla. Fold in the flour mixture a little at a time. Just before completed, fold in the coconut, chocolate, and pecans. Drop 2 tablespoons of dough on your lined cookie sheet about 2-inches apart. Bake for about 15 minutes. Cool on a wire rack.

Lemon Ricotta Cookies

Makes 2 dozen

I use lemon whenever possible in any kind of recipe, and find that my favorite desserts usually contain lemon. If you like Italian ricotta cookies, you have to try them with lemon added. I used to buy them whenever I went to the Italian grocery. I actually didn't learn how to make them until I was an adult.

Story by Monica

2½ cups all-purpose flour
1 teaspoon baking powder
1 teaspoon salt
½ stick butter, softened
2 cups sugar
2 eggs
1 (15 oz.) container whole milk ricotta cheese
3 tablespoons lemon juice
Zest of 1 lemon

Icing

1½ cups powdered sugar
4 tablespoons lemon juice
Zest of 1 lemon

Preheat an oven to 375°F. Line two baking pans with parchment paper.

In a medium bowl, combine the flour, baking powder, and salt. In another bowl, mix the butter and sugar, and beat until fluffy. Add eggs one at a time, beating until mixed in. Add the ricotta, lemon juice, and zest, and continue to beat. Add in the dry ingredients. Drop 2 tablespoons per cookie onto the prepared baking sheets. Bake for 15 minutes or until slightly golden at the edges. After removing from the oven, allow to rest on the baking sheets for 20 minutes.

Icing

In a small bowl, combine all the ingredients and stir until smooth. Spoon onto each cookie and gently spread (it will take about 2 hours for the glaze to harden).

Lemon Meringue Pie

Serves 8

1 (9-inch) pie shell, baked

Filling
1 cup sugar
¼ cup cornstarch
1 cup boiling water
1 tablespoon unsalted butter
3 eggs, separated and beaten lightly
Zest of 1 lemon
¼ cup freshly squeezed lemon juice

Meringue
3 egg whites
¼ teaspoon cream of tartar
6 tablespoons sugar

Filling

Mix the sugar and cornstarch. Add boiling water slowly, and boil over low heat, stirring constantly until clear. Add the butter and egg yolks. Cook in a double-boiler until it gets thick, stirring constantly. Add lemon zest and juice. Cool (egg whites will be used in the meringue). Fold half of the meringue into the filling mixture, and fill the pie shell. Cover with the remaining meringue, and bake at 300°F for 15 to 20 minutes.

Meringue

Beat the egg whites (set aside from the filling ingredients) with cream of tartar until frothy. Beat in the sugar gradually. Continue beating until the mixture is stiff (the sugar should be fully dissolved). Swirl the other half of the meringue over the pie filling, lifting your spatula to form peaks. Bake as indicated above.

Lemon Layer Cake

Serves 10-12

Cake

½ cup butter

1 cup sugar

4 egg yolks

½ teaspoon vanilla

½ teaspoon lemon extract

2 cups cake flour

3 teaspoons baking powder

½ cup milk

Filling

4 eggs

2 cups sugar

1 cup water

2 lemons, grated rind and juice

Icing

1 lemon, grated rind

2 tablespoons lemon juice

2 tablespoons boiling water

2 cups confectioners' sugar

Cake

Preheat an oven to 350°F. Cream the butter, add sugar, and beat. Add lightly beaten egg yolks, vanilla, and lemon extract, and mix thoroughly. Sift the flour and baking powder, and add alternately with milk. Beat and place in three (8-inch) greased and floured pans. Bake for 35 minutes or until it rises, becomes lightly browned, and shrinks from the sides of the pan. Cool on a wire rack.

Filling

Beat the eggs. Boil the sugar and water until it makes a syrup. Add the lemon rind and juice, then add the eggs. Boil all together for 20 minutes, stirring well. When the cake is partially cooled, spread the filling between the layers that have been cut to size.

Icing

Add lemon rind to juice and water. Stir in the sugar a little at a time. Spread the icing on the top and sides of the cake. Garnish with fresh raspberries (optional).

Rugelach

Harry Myers *(Lipan, TX)*
Makes 1 dozen

> These tasty cream cheese crescent cookies are festive and memorable. They are a perfect outlet for your creativity. The endless sweet fillings are limited by your imagination. Once you bake them, you will ponder the next batch, and experiment with different fillings.

1 cup unsalted butter (or margarine)
1 (8 oz.) package cream cheese
2 cups all-purpose flour
¼ teaspoon salt
⅓ cup sour cream
½ cup white sugar
1 tablespoon ground cinnamon
1 cup finely chopped walnuts
½ cup raisins, finely chopped

Cut the cold butter or margarine and cream cheese into bits. In a food processor, pulse the flour, salt, butter (or margarine), cream cheese, and sour cream until crumbly. Shape the crumbly mixture into four equal disks. Wrap each disk, and chill for 2 hours or up to 2 days. Roll each disk into a 9-inch round, keeping the other disks chilled until ready to roll. Combine the sugar, cinnamon, chopped walnuts, and finely chopped raisins (may substitute miniature chocolate chips for raisins). Roll each disk into a 9-inch round, keeping the other disks chilled until ready to roll. Sprinkle the rounds with the sugar-nut mixture. Press lightly into the dough. With a chef's knife or pizza cutter, cut each round into 12 wedges. Roll the wedges from wide to narrow (you will end up with a point on the outside of each cookie). Place on ungreased baking sheets, and chill the rugelach for 20 minutes before baking. Preheat an oven to 350°F. After the rugelach are chilled, bake them in the center rack of your oven for 22 minutes or until lightly golden. Cool on wire racks. Store in airtight containers (they freeze very well).

Before putting the filling on the dough, use a pastry brush to layer apricot jam as well as brown sugar, then adding the recommended filling. You may also make a mixture of cinnamon and sugar, and roll the rugelach in this prior to putting them on the cookie sheets.

Chocolate Silk Cake with Candied Cranberries

Celeste Morin *(Centerport, NY)*
Serves 10

My cousin Bob's wife, Celeste, made this cake for a Christmas party one year. The red berries glistened in the candlelight, and we couldn't wait to try it. Celeste is known in the family for her delicious and creative baking expertise. Celeste's mom had been a great cook, but hadn't baked, so Celeste and her sister took up an interest in baking. With regard to her cooking, she has said of herself that she actually can't make a decent egg, but she can make a fabulous soufflé because her first introduction to serious cooking came straight from two enormous volumes of Jacques Pepin's *The Art of Cooking,* from which she carefully followed the gourmet recipes to every detail, resulting in beautiful, sophisticated dishes.

Story by Monica

Crust
2 cups graham cracker crumbs
6 tablespoons unsalted butter, melted

Filling
8 ounces bittersweet or semisweet chocolate, chopped
⅓ cup milk
⅓ cup half-and-half
⅓ cup coffee-flavored liqueur (such as Kahlúa®)
1 cup (2 sticks) unsalted butter, room temperature
5 large egg yolks
3 tablespoons light corn syrup

Candied Cranberries
1 (12 oz.) package frozen cranberries, unthawed
1 cup sugar

Crust

Preheat an oven to 350°F. Stir the graham cracker crumbs in a bowl with the butter until combined. Press the mixture onto the bottom and sides of a 9-inch springform pan with 2¾-inch sides. Freeze for 15 minutes.

Filling

Combine the chocolate, milk, half-and-half, and liqueur in a heavy, large saucepan. Stir over medium heat until the chocolate melts and the mixture is smooth. Gradually add butter, stirring until melted. Whisk the egg yolks in a large bowl. Gradually combine the chocolate mixture and corn syrup. Pour the filling into the prepared crust. Bake until the filling begins to bubble (about 15 minutes). Transfer to a rack and cool. Cover and refrigerate overnight.

Candied Cranberries

Preheat an oven to 375°F. Spray a rimmed baking sheet with nonstick spray. Toss the cranberries and sugar in a medium bowl to blend. Spread out the mixture on the baking sheet, and bake for 10 minutes. Using a metal spatula, stir the berries gently. Bake until the berries are thawed and most of the sugar is dissolved (about 5 minutes). Cool to room temperature, reserving the syrupy liquid for later use, and place the cold berries onto the cake. Drizzle with berry syrup (the remaining liquid from cooking down the berries). Chill again before serving.

This is also a great recipe for summer: just replace the cranberries with 3½ pints of raspberries, 1 pint of sliced strawberries, and 3 tablespoons of raspberry jam. Melt the jam, and pour over the berries.

Chocolate Cream Puffs

Serves 4

½ cup plus 2 tablespoons butter
1 cup hot water
1 cup flour
4 eggs

Filling
1 cup heavy cream
⅛-¼ cup semisweet chocolate
1 teaspoon vanilla
Pinch salt
⅛ teaspoon sugar

Preheat an oven to 375°F. Boil ½ cup of butter with the hot water. When boiling, stir in the flour, stirring until it thickens and leaves the sides of the pan. Remove from the stove, and add eggs one at a time, beating hard after each one is added. Drop the mixture by the tablespoon onto a buttered baking sheet. Bake for about 45 minutes. Cool on a wire rack. Once cooked, split open and fill.

Filling

Beat the cream until stiff. Flavor with melted chocolate, vanilla, a pinch of salt, and sugar. Mix together and fill.

Shaker Cookies

Makes 1 dozen

1½ cups brown sugar
1 tablespoon shortening
1 egg, lightly beaten
Pinch salt
2 cups uncooked oat flakes
2 teaspoons baking powder
1 cup cake flour
2 teaspoons cinnamon
½ cup chopped raisins
1 cup milk

Preheat an oven to 350°F. Mix the sugar and shortening, then add the egg. Sift the remaining dry ingredients. Add the sifted dry ingredients alternately with the milk. Drop by the teaspoon on a greased cookie sheet 1-inch apart. Bake for 12 to 15 minutes.

Homemade Gingersnaps

Rita McKittrick *(Middle Island, NY)*
Yield 3-4 dozen

1½ cups shortening
1¾ cups sugar, divided
2 eggs
½ cup molasses
4 cups flour
2 teaspoons baking soda
2 teaspoons ground ginger

Preheat an oven to 350°F. Cream the shortening, 1¼ cups of sugar, eggs, and molasses. Sift the dry ingredients, and add to the creamed mixture. Chill. Roll into balls. Dip in the remaining sugar. Place on a lightly greased cookie sheet. Bake for 12 to 15 minutes. Cool on a bakers' rack.

Grandma LaCapria's Butter Cookies

Loren Christie *(Patchogue, NY)*
Serves 25
Makes 3 dozen

5 cups flour
2 cups sugar
1 tablespoon baking powder
5 eggs
2 sticks butter, softened
Sprinkles, to garnish

Preheat an oven to 425°F. Mix the flour, sugar, and baking powder. Dump the mixture onto a large cookie sheet. Make a hole in the middle, and crack the eggs into it. Add butter into the hole. Squish into the dough. Roll out and cut into shapes. Bake on a greased cookie sheet for 8 to 10 minutes. Shake on the sprinkles right out of the oven when they are warm.

Vegan Cupcakes

Liz Finnegan *(Islip, NY)*
Serves 12

1 cup soy milk
1 tablespoon apple cider vinegar
¾ cup sugar
⅓ cup canola oil
1½ teaspoons vanilla extract
1 cup all-purpose flour
¼ teaspoon baking soda
½ teaspoon baking powder
¼ teaspoon salt

Preheat an oven to 350°F. Line a muffin tin with paper cups. Whisk the soy milk and vinegar, and set aside for several minutes. Add the sugar, oil, and vanilla extract, and beat until it is foamy. In a separate bowl, sift the dry ingredients. Add to the wet ingredients, and beat until mostly smooth. Fill cups three-quarters, and bake for 15 to 20 minutes or until a toothpick comes out clean. Cool on a wire rack. Ice with your favorite frosting (see page 188).

▎ To make chocolate cupcakes, add ⅓ cup of cocoa powder.

Black Bottom Cupcakes

Liz Finnegan *(Islip, NY)*
Makes 20-24

When the kids were little, they thought that the slice-and-bake chocolate chip cookies purchased in the grocery store were just the best. Of course, that was a time when Mommy could do no wrong, and I was pretty much the center of their universe. Yet, one day, my eldest son (then nine years old) asked for my help on a project that could have shattered that image.

The public library was running a baking contest for elementary-aged kids, and he wanted to be in it. The only thing that he needed was a sure-fire cookie or cake recipe to wow the judges. I was frozen in fear: even the least-sophisticated judging palates would be able to tell the difference between baked-from-scratch and Pillsbury®.

Alas, karma prevailed, and the very next day, one of my favorite morning talk shows interviewed a baker who shared some of her favorite recipes, among them being the Black Bottom Cupcakes. I quickly copied the recipe, ran out and bought the ingredients, and, by the time both boys were home from school, I was ready to help him meet the challenge.

1½ cups flour
1 cup sugar
¼ cup cocoa
½ teaspoon salt
1 teaspoon baking soda
1 cup water
⅓ cup oil
1 teaspoon vanilla
1 tablespoon white vinegar
⅓ cup sugar
1 egg
8 ounces softened cream cheese
6 ounces chocolate chips

Mix the flour, sugar, cocoa, salt, baking soda, water, oil, vanilla, and vinegar in a bowl, and beat 350 strokes by hand.

In a separate bowl, cream the sugar, egg, cream cheese, and chocolate chips.

Fill a cupcake tin two-thirds full with the first batter. Spoon the second batter on top. Bake for 20 to 25 minutes.

Tips for a Well-Stocked Pantry

It is always best to use fresh fruits, vegetables, meats, and fish, but in a pinch, you may have to rely on your stored ingredients. Try to keep the following items stocked in your pantry, refrigerator, and freezer so you can cook up a tasty and healthy meal or dessert any time. It is also a good idea to stock up when these items are on sale at your supermarket. Always remember to check the expiration date on sale items.

Basics for a Quick Meal or Dessert

In the Pantry: Whole-wheat pasta (different shapes and sizes); different kinds of rice, oatmeal, and other cereals; seasoned bread crumbs; stuffing mix; several varieties of beans (dried and canned); canned tomatoes (whole, crushed, pureed, and paste); teriyaki sauce; Gravy-Master®; chicken and beef stocks; canned milk; dried mushrooms; various nuts; different kinds of flour (all-purpose white, whole-wheat, rye, cake, gluten-free blends, and rice); sugars (brown [dark and light], raw, white, confectioners', and decorator); molasses; honey; artificial sweetener (like stevia); baking soda and baking powder; active dry yeast packets; vanilla (and other essences like lemon and orange); chocolate chips (plus caramel and peanut butter chips); chocolate bars; dried fruits (raisins, cherries, cranberries, apricots, pineapple, and mango); peanut butter; and sprinkles

Dried Spices: Ground cinnamon, nutmeg, garlic and onion powders and pieces, crystallized and ground ginger, chili powder, paprika, mustard, cumin, whole and ground cloves, curry powder, garam masala, coriander, and different kinds of salt and pepper

Dried Herbs: Oregano, parsley, dill, ground and whole rosemary, basil, cilantro, mint, sage, bay leaves, thyme, and lemon thyme

In the Freezer: Several kinds of vegetables and fruits (including peppers, onions, celery, cherries, berries, bananas, raspberries, and peaches), frozen juices from citrus fruits kept in ice trays, pizza dough, cheese, butter, cookie dough, leftover stock (vegetable, fish, and chicken), sauces, bits of meats, peeled shrimp, and fish fillets

In the Refrigerator: Lemon, lime, and orange juice; any leftovers from open bottles of wine; beer and champagne to use in recipes; capers; relish; sun-dried tomatoes; olives; horseradish; marmalade and jams; milk; eggs; butter; and a variety of bottled sauces for flavoring (including chili sauce, hoisin, teriyaki, soy, and barbecue)

Growing Your Own Herbs

Most of us are ambitious gardeners, and we end up buying and growing more herbs than we can possibly use. So, before you start planting, be sure to carefully plan how much you will need to grow.

Here is a sampling of the basics for every herb garden: basil, chives, coriander (also known as cilantro), dill, mint, oregano, parsley, rosemary, and thyme. Note that one tablespoon of fresh, chopped herbs is equivalent to a half-teaspoon of dried, crushed herbs.

Toward the end of your garden's growing season, you must be vigilant regarding frost. Keep an eye on the weather reports, because a light frost will appear at 32°F. If frost is predicted, and you are not prepared to finally harvest your garden, break out the blankets and sheets, and cover your plants, vegetables, and flowers the night before, then uncovering them in the morning once the sun has come out. If some of your vegetables are affected by the light frost, you can sometimes save them by hosing them down early in the morning before the sun hits them. At the first reports of frost, it is best to harvest all of your sensitive vegetables, such as tomatoes, peppers, eggplant, and basil. You can put your unripe green tomatoes in a paper bag in a dark environment, and they will ripen shortly thereafter. You can typically keep flowers out a little longer if your carefully cover them each night. Parsley, pumpkins, and rosemary are more likely to withstand the frost until Thanksgiving, because they are hardier.

Once you have harvested your herbs, you will need to decide whether you will be using them within the next week. For the short-term storage of basil, parsley, and cilantro, you can trim the ends and place in a glass with an inch of water on the counter at room temperature for up to a week, clipping for use each time that you need them. For chives, thyme, and rosemary, loosely cover the un-rinsed herbs in plastic wrap, and place in the warmest part of the refrigerator or in a large plastic bag with a crumpled paper towel. Rinse them immediately before using.

If you will not be using your herbs right away, they can be dried for future use. To dry, either place chopped basil, parsley leaves, or whole thyme or rosemary on a plate. Set aside in a cool, dry place for several days, and then store them in a plastic container in the freezer or refrigerator. You can also make small bouquets of herbs tied with ribbon or string, and hang them upside-down to dry. Then store them as mentioned above or display them in your kitchen for a homey touch. Use your frozen herbs right up until your next growing season.

Growing Your Own Food

Healthy living does not mean giving up good food and great flavor. Simply eating unprocessed food and employing healthy cooking methods will put you on track for better overall health. Serving fresh garlic, green, leafy vegetables (like spinach and kale) and herbs (like basil and parsley), and using extra-virgin olive oil for sautéing and salad dressings are all great ways to improve and maintain a healthier lifestyle.

Growing some of your own vegetables and fruits has the added benefits of saving money and increasing quality family time by working together in the garden. Blueberries and raspberries are easy to grow, and can be great options for beginning gardeners. In warmer climates, citrus fruits grow in many backyards. My Italian garden is comprised of herbs such as oregano, basil, and parsley, along with cherry, plum, and beefsteak tomatoes, eggplant, green and red peppers, and zucchini. We eat what is most plentiful as it is picked, and then prepare and freeze the rest for future use.

It is important to pick at just the right time to elicit the maximum flavor, texture, and nutritive value. You can get the most vitamins and minerals from your produce by using them as soon after harvesting as possible. Essential vitamins and minerals enable our bodies to function properly, which helps us to live longer, more productive lives. It is also important to properly store your precious fruits and vegetables, being careful not to bruise them while picking because they will spoil more quickly.

Baking Tips

We know practice makes perfect in everything we attempt to master, so you may have to bake a few cakes before you can deem them ready to serve to anyone. Although baking is a science in which precise measuring is tantamount to a good result, no science is perfect. A lopsided cake or a quiche that isn't done in the middle is a distinct possibility unless you know what to look for. Here are a few tips to help develop your baking expertise.

As with all aspects of cooking and baking, try to use the freshest possible ingredients. When making brownies, use the best chocolate available. For fruit pies, try to choose fresh-picked fruit over frozen, and if fresh-picked is not available, use frozen over canned to cut down on sugar, salt, and over-processing. When baking bread, check the expiration date on your yeast to ensure that it is still usable. Replenish baking soda and baking powder regularly for best results.

Set up all of your necessary ingredients before embarking on any baking project. It can be a real disappointment to find that you've thrown out the egg whites because the recipe called for yolks, only to find that it calls for egg whites at the end of the recipe. Have all your ingredients at room temperature unless your recipe requires them to be cold. For instance, eggs are easiest to separate when cold, although egg whites whip up best at room temperature.

There are stages to every recipe. Once you have set out your ingredients, next prepare to bake by readying your equipment. Before you mix up your batter, grease your pans. Butter is always a better choice than any other fat in your cake recipes, because it gives the richest flavor and, when used in moderation, it is a fine choice. When softening butter, try slicing it before adding to your recipe to speed up the process. On the other hand, when baking bread, shortening is your best choice, because it absorbs into the batter less than butter will. When greasing your pans, use a pastry brush so the butter, shortening, or oil is more evenly distributed. When necessary, also dust the greased pans with flour to reduce sticking. Next, check to see if your recipe requires the oven to be preheated. You should preheat the oven to the required temperature about 15 minutes before you are ready to bake.

Even if your recipe doesn't call for sifting your dry ingredients, I tend to do it, anyway, so everything is fully mixed. I have even used a small hand-held strainer to sift, which is quick and easy. Since most of my baking projects are given away or for special occasions, I am always in a hurry to finish them and have time to gift wrap or decorate, so hand-held is always easier than a bigger apparatus like a sifter for me. There aren't too many shortcuts when baking, so I take advantage of them whenever I can.

When making tea-breads like banana bread or applesauce loaves, both of which use chopped nuts, I use the following shortcut for chopping nuts. Fill a plastic bag with the nuts, and hammer them with a kitchen mallet. It is a quick and neat way to chop your nuts without lugging out the food processor. I always add in the nuts and fruits last, unless the recipe states otherwise. I like to make sure that my batter is fully mixed before adding them, and they will be less likely to bleed into the batter if thrown in last. When mixing, always scrape down the sides and up from the bottom of your bowl using a rubber spatula to completely mix in every drop.

It is important to be precise when mixing, especially when measuring. Whenever baking a large batch of cupcakes, cookies, or cakes, always measure the exact amount for each one using a tablespoon or measuring cups so they all have a consistent texture. Make sure that your flour is fully blended so the cake rises evenly. Be sure not to overfill your pans, as they will overflow, making your cake lopsided (I suggest filling your pans no more than two-thirds). To be most precise, you may want to use a kitchen scale to measure your ingredients or each portion to be baked.

You've laid out your ingredients, having carefully measured and mixed, but find that your cake has dropped, meaning that the middle has fallen in. There may be a couple of reasons why. Do not open the oven door before it is time, as this can result in your cake being undercooked. In my house, we don't even walk into the kitchen when a cake is baking, because we don't want to be tempted to open the oven. If you find that your cake has cracked too much, your oven may be too hot or low, or because the fruit used in your recipe sank to the bottom before it was set in place. Never allow your pan to touch the sides of the oven, or one side of your cake will end up being dry and overdone because the air can't circulate evenly around it. Always use the center rack of your oven and bake in smaller batches, if necessary. It may take more time, but the end result is rewarding.

Oven temperatures vary, so it is important to know how to tell when what you've baked is done. You'll need to call upon your senses and good old common sense by looking, touching, or smelling. Here are just a few ways to test for doneness. Your cake is done when a skewer or toothpick comes out clean when inserted in the center. You can also tell it is done, because the scent of it baking will fully permeate the air of your kitchen. Other clues are that pastries will be lightly browned, bread will give a hollow sound when tapped, and muffins will spring back when gently touched.

Allow cakes and cookies to cool completely. Always use a baker's rack to cool your cakes and cookies to allow air flow on the bottom as well as the top. This will also prevent your baked goods from overbaking. After 10 minutes, you should be able to turn them out onto a flat surface (such as a counter, plate, or platter) to finish cooling. There is nothing worse than having your cake stuck to the bottom of the pan. If you have trouble getting your cake out, use a dampened dishtowel, and set the cake on it to loosen it up before turning out. Allow them to cool for about one hour before icing, frosting, or any other decorating.

Never frost your baked goods right from the oven. We do not often just take the cake out of the oven, cool it, and frost it. There is usually a fair amount of primping and trimming required to achieve that perfect look. Before frosting your cake, cut it into the shape that you will be using. If it is a layer cake, do you want it more round? Trim around the edges to make every layer a consistent size. If you are making a theme cake, you will have to trim the cake to suit your design (this can be done using a serrated knife). Take the time to chill the cake for 30 minutes to an hour for easier spreading of the frosting. First apply a thin layer of frosting, and then chill again before the final frosting of the entire cake to help conceal any crumbs.

All-Purpose White Cake

½ cup butter
1 cup sugar
2 cups cake flour
3 teaspoons baking powder
⅔ cup milk
½ teaspoon almond extract
Zest of 1 lemon
3 egg whites

Preheat an oven to 350°F. Cream the butter, add sugar, and continue beating. Sift the flour, then sift three more times with baking powder, and add to the butter mixture alternately with milk. Beat thoroughly until smooth, and add almond extract and lemon zest. Fold in the egg whites (beaten stiff, but not dry). Butter and flour a 12- x 8-inch pan. Pour your batter into the pan and bake for about 1 hour. To make two layers, bake in two greased and floured 9-inch layer pans at 375°F for 25 to 30 minutes. Fill and frost with your favorite icing.

Icings and Frostings

Chocolate Frosting

1 (3 oz.) package cream cheese
2 tablespoons milk
2 cups confectioners' sugar
⅛ teaspoon salt
1 teaspoon vanilla
2 squares semisweet chocolate, melted

Cream the cream cheese, and add milk slowly. Beat in the confectioners' sugar a little at a time until all is absorbed and the mixture becomes smooth. Add salt, vanilla, and chocolate. Blend well and ice the cake. This will frost a 13- x 9-inch cake. You can also double this recipe to make enough frosting to fill a layer cake.

White Frosting

1¼ cup white corn syrup
2 egg whites
⅛ teaspoon salt
1 teaspoon vanilla

Heat the corn syrup to boiling. Combine the unbeaten egg whites, salt, and vanilla in a large bowl, and beat using an electric mixer at high speed until the egg whites are stiff. Slowly pour in the boiled syrup, and continue to beat until the frosting is fluffy and hangs in peaks from your beater. This will frost a 13- x 9-inch cake. You can also double this recipe to make enough frosting to fill a layer cake.

Rocky Road Frosting

2⅔ cups sifted confectioners' sugar
⅓ cup cocoa
⅓ cup butter, softened
3-4 tablespoons milk
1 cup miniature marshmallows
½ cup salted peanuts

Sift the sugar and cocoa together, and then blend in the butter and milk. Stir in the marshmallows and peanuts. This will frost a 13- x 9-inch cake. You can also double this recipe to make enough frosting to fill a layer cake.

White Mountain Icing

Nora Rooney *(Raleigh, NC)*

> This recipe was given to me by my old boyfriend's mom when she made it for her husband's birthday party. It was fantastic, so I made sure to request the recipe from her so I could make it on my own.

½ cup sugar
¼ cup white corn syrup
2 tablespoons water
1 teaspoon vanilla

Blend the sugar, syrup, and water, and boil rapidly until the mixture spins to ⅙ to ⅛-inch thread. Beat egg whites until peaks form. Pour the sugar mixture into the egg whites in a steady stream, beating constantly until the icing stands up in very stiff peaks. Blend in the vanilla, and spread on the cake.

Coconut Topping

1 coconut (including the milk)
¾ cup milk
¾ cup sugar

Grate the coconut. Add coconut milk, regular milk, and sugar. Heat until there is a change in color, and then spread onto the cake.

About Muffins

If using a different size muffin tin than the recipe calls for, follow this simple rule of thumb to change the baking time: increase the baking time if using larger muffin tins and decrease baking for smaller muffin tins (the difference in time is usually about 10 minutes).

It is much prettier and cleaner to use muffin liners. They come in so many beautiful seasonal colors and designs that you're sure to find the perfect one to brighten any type of muffin. Before baking, fill any empty muffin cups with a few tablespoons of water to keep the pan from warping due to high temperatures hitting the empty cups. If your muffins are sticking to the bottom of the pan, place the entire tin on a wet towel for a few minutes to loosen them. To make a more heart-healthy muffin, try using two egg whites in place of one whole egg, which leaves out the yolk. To cut the fat in a recipe, try using ¾ cups of applesauce with ¼ cup of extra-virgin olive oil instead of a full cup of oil.

Various Muffin Tin Sizes
(Typically 6-, 12-, or 24-cup sizes)

Standard Muffin Cup: 2½ inches in diameter. Holds ¼ to ⅓ cup batter.

Giant Muffin Cup: 3¼ inches in diameter. Holds ⅝ cups of batter.

Mini-Muffin Cup: 1½ inches to 2 inches in diameter. Holds ⅛ cup or 2 full tablespoons of batter.

About Pastry

When mixing your dough ingredients, it is best to keep them chilled. Measure your flour and salt into a chilled bowl, and quickly work in the shortening. Cover the dough and chill for at least 30 minutes before rolling it out.

To roll your dough, lightly dust a flat surface with flour. You can also roll out your dough between two sheets of waxed paper. Generally, dough should be rolled 1/8- to ¼-inch thick.

For a two-crust pie, divide your dough into two portions. Keep the portion designated for the bottom crust slightly larger to be fit into the bottom of your pie plate (you can trim the edges if it overhangs too much, and dab with a bit of water to maintain firmness). After adding your top crust, trim any extra pastry around the edges, fold the edge of the top crust under the edge of the lower crust, and secure with your fingertips or a fork. Prick holes in the top for ventilation during baking.

To make a lattice top, start by placing the bottom crust loosely in the pie plate. Trim and roll out the rest of the pastry. Cut ½-inch strips using your pastry wheel, and place in a criss-cross fashion over the filled pie, laying down first in one direction, and then the other to overlap and weave in and out of the first layer of strips. Fold the edge of your bottom crust over the strips after moistening with water to help adhere it in place, then pressing to seal using your fingertips or a fork.

Quick Pastry

Makes 1 9-inch pie crust

½ cup shortening
¼ cup cold water
1½ cups flour
½ teaspoon baking powder
½ teaspoon salt

Melt the shortening. Add water, and mix with the remaining ingredients to form a smooth dough. Chill before rolling out on a floured surface. Use in your recipe as directed above.

Puff Pastry

5 cups bread flour
2½ teaspoons salt
2 cups water (or as needed)
2 cups unsalted butter, room temperature

Mix the flour and salt together in a large bowl, and stir in the water a little at a time. The dough should hold together just enough to leave the sides of the bowl (use only enough water to achieve this consistency). Shape into a ball and let rest for 10 minutes. Next, place butter between two sheets of plastic wrap, pound into a disc, and refrigerate for 20 minutes or until firm. Lightly flour your work surface and roll out the dough into a large rectangle until about ½-inch thick. Place the chilled disc of butter in the center, and fold the two ends over so the butter is covered by the dough. Roll out the dough again, taking care not to let the butter break through. Roll to ½-inch thick. Fold into thirds like a jelly roll. Roll out, again, into a rectangle. As the butter starts to warm, wrap and refrigerate, again, for 30 minutes. Repeat the rolling twice more as before. The dough should now be ice cold and ready to use in your recipe. Bake in a hot oven (400-500°F), turning the dough several times for even distribution of heat.

To make individual puff pastry tarts, roll the dough as thin as ¼ inch. Cut rounds of the pastry, and cover the backs of muffin tins or custard cups, pleating the edges to fit. Prick the dough several times to ventilate, bake at 500°F until risen, and then at 350°F until browned. Cool and fill.

Puff pastry pie shells require rolling half of the pastry enough to fit over the back of a pie plate. Trim the excess dough, pleat the edges to fit, prick to ventilate, and bake as with tarts above. Cool and fill.

Crust Alternatives

Vanilla Wafer Crust

1½ cups vanilla wafers, pulverized
4 tablespoons butter, melted
2 tablespoons sugar

Mix all the ingredients and press into a greased 9-inch pie plate, making sure to cover the bottom and up the sides. Bake at 350°F for 10 minutes, cool, and fill.

Gingersnap Crust

1½ cups gingersnaps, pulverized
¼ cup flour
4 tablespoons melted butter

Mix all the ingredients and press into a greased 9-inch pie plate, making sure to cover the bottom and up the sides. Bake at 350°F for 10 minutes, cool, and fill.

Pecan Crust

2½ cups pecans, halved
¼ cup light brown sugar
4 tablespoons melted butter

Mix all the ingredients and press into a greased 9-inch pie plate, making sure to cover the bottom and up the sides. Bake at 375°F for 15 to 20 minutes, cool, and fill.

Graham Cracker Crust

10 graham crackers, crushed
¼ cup confectioners' sugar
5 tablespoons melted butter

Mix all the ingredients and press into a greased 9-inch pie plate, making sure to cover the bottom and up the sides. Bake for 10 minutes in a 350°F oven.

About Cookies

Unless your recipe states otherwise, always grease your cookie sheets lightly. Have several cookie sheets available to bake more than one batch at a time. While one batch is in the oven, you can be preparing the next batch. Wipe the baking sheet clean and grease, again, between each batch.

Use a melon baller or teaspoon to accurately measure out each cookie to be baked. You may bake them softer or crispier in consistency. For a softer cookie, take it out of the oven 1 to 2 minutes before the required time. For a crispier cookie, bake until browned very lightly and evenly. You can also thin the dough slightly by adding a bit more liquid so the cookie spreads out thinner on the sheet. Experiment with one or two cookies to reach your desired consistency.

Always allow cookies to cool on baking racks. Do not overlap cookies; let them cool flat. To store soft cookies, use an airtight container. For crisp cookies, use a jar that permits airflow. Around the holidays, storing cookies is a necessity, because they are often used as gifts. Check to see which of your cookies can be frozen. To freeze, store the cookies in a large tin lined with waxed paper. They can be frozen like this for a few weeks throughout the holidays and served as needed.

Rolled Cookies

As with all dough to be rolled, it should be sufficiently chilled before attempting to handle. Roll on a floured surface one batch at a time. For crispier cookies, roll the dough as thin as possible (the thicker the dough, the softer the cookie will be). You can also use cookie cutters to make interesting shapes. Try using cardboard and a sharp knife to cut out your own patterns.

Drop Cookies

Dough for drop cookies cannot be molded or used with cookie cutters, because it is too thick. To ensure consistent size and baking time, use a teaspoon or a melon baller to scoop up the dough, and drop it onto your greased cookie sheet. Oatmeal and chocolate chip cookies are done this way. Drop the cookies at least two inches apart, as they will spread while baking. Cool on a bakers rack.

About Bread

Most of the sliced breads sold in our supermarkets and bakeries (such as white, rye, and whole- wheat) are yeast breads. These need yeast in order to activate the dough. This bread can be baked in loaves, as rolls, or shaped and seasoned in a wide variety of ways. The more cake-like breads, called "quick breads" or "tea breads," use baking powder or baking soda.

Yeast Breads

The two kinds of yeast most often used in a home kitchen are cake yeast and active dry yeast. The packaged dry yeast is equal to one cake yeast. They both need to be activated using ¼ cup of warm liquid, as you will find in many of the recipes in this book. Cake yeast must be refrigerated before use, but the packaged dry yeast can be stored in your pantry.

Once you have activated the yeast (which takes three to five minutes), you can make either a straight dough, where all the flour is added to make a stiff dough; a sponge dough, where a sponge is made first with liquids, yeast, and part of the flour, and allowed to rise before adding the rest of the flour to make your stiff dough; or a mixer dough, where you blend the yeast with other dry ingredients using half of the flour. Add in the necessary liquid (¼ cup of water may be substituted for whichever liquid is listed in the recipe) and warmed shortening. Add this to the dry ingredients, followed by eggs, and beat for three minutes at a low speed until fully moistened. Stir in any remaining flour and fruits or nuts, and then knead and let rise as indicated in your recipe.

Always knead dough on a floured surface. It will be ready when it is smooth, elastic, and springs back when touched. After kneading, the dough then needs time to rise. Place it into a greased bowl and coat all sides with grease. Let it rise at room temperature, and once it has doubled in size, punch it down and let it rise, again (the dough should double in bulk).

To shape loaves, roll out the dough like a jelly roll, and pinch the edges to seal it. Place the roll seam-side down into a standard loaf pan (5- x 9-inch or 4½- x 8½-inch). The dough should reach halfway up the pan. Cover, again, and let it rise above the pan .You are then ready to bake per your recipe instructions. You will know when it is perfectly baked if the loaf makes a hollow sound when tapped lightly. Remove your fresh bread from the pan and cool on a bakers rack.

Tea Breads
Tea breads are delicious when warm and served on their own or with butter, cream cheese, or preserves.You may also enjoy them along with a meal served in a bread basket (such as pumpkin bread at Thanksgiving).The major difference between tea breads and yeast breads is the time it takes for the bread to rise, also known as the leavening process.Tea breads rise in the oven through the use of either baking powder or baking soda, both of which are activated by the heat of the oven during the baking process. There is no kneading like in a yeast-based bread or separating of eggs as in many cake recipes. They take no more than 10 minutes of prep work and an hour to bake. They are sometimes called "quick breads" and are most often baked in loaves, but can be made into muffins or layer cakes by altering the baking time for the type of pan you are using.

Baking Tools

- baking/cookie sheets (at least two)
- bread loaf pan (at least two)
- cake pans (several sizes)
- candy thermometer
- convection oven
- cutting boards (several sizes; one wood and one plastic)
- cookie cutters (varied shapes and seasonal themes)
- cookie scoopers
- electric mixer
- hand mixer
- hand sifter
- hot pad and oven mitts
- individual ramekins (at least eight)
- jelly-roll pan
- kitchen shears
- kitchen timer
- measuring cups (three sizes)
- measuring spoons (at least two sets; one plastic and one metal)
- mixing bowls (small, medium, large, and extra-large)
- muffin pans (standard, giant, and mini)
- pastry blender
- pastry brush
- pastry crimping wheel/pastry cutter
- pie plates/pie pans
- pie weights
- rolling pin, pastry cloth, and rolling pin cover
- spatulas (several sizes; plastic, metal, and nonstick)
- tart molds
- oven thermometer
- toothpicks or skewers
- wire cooling racks (at least two)
- wire whisk (several sizes)
- wooden spoons (several sizes)
- zester

Menu Planner

I think that one of the most commonly asked daily questions is, "What should we have for dinner?" The next most important question is, "What's for dessert?" (especially when it comes to my son). I hear it all the time at work, and it is often discussed endlessly with friends and neighbors. Every day, it is a new dilemma. We want to make something interesting instead of having the same thing every week. Can I also find time to make a cake or brownies for dessert?

Planning a weekly menu saves time and money. My local supermarket circulars come out on a Thursday, so I always browse through them to get an idea of what is on sale. I then clip whatever coupons that I can use, and bring along any recipes that I am thinking of preparing. Checking the refrigerator and pantry before you go to the store saves a lot of guesswork as to what you will need. Picking what vegetables and fruits are ripe in the garden will also determine what you shop for, inspiring you to choose items that will enable you to use your harvested gems.

When planning my weekly menu, I often will scan my recipe boxes. I keep several recipe boxes: one from my mother-in-law, Mary, another with recipes that I have created or gotten from friends, and a third with recipes that I have clipped out of newspapers and magazines.

In the supermarket, don't forget to pick up any yeast packets for your cinnamon buns or breads, and grab some frozen pie crusts in case you don't have enough time to make your own crusts (you can find very good choices in the frozen foods section of most supermarkets). Shop for a varied menu, including chicken, chopped sirloin, and a third meat of your choice. If the store is having a good sale, I will sometimes buy extra meat and freeze it. I also buy several kinds of green, leafy vegetables (like spinach, broccoli, and kale), because they are vegetable staples in my house. Other vegetables (like carrots, celery, potatoes, and onions) should carry over from week to week, and will only need to be replenished when necessary. Of course, also be sure to look in your refrigerator before going to the store to check if other staples (like milk, eggs, and butter) need to be bought. I also make a stop at my local farm stand to see what fresh produce that they have that I may not have grown in my garden, such as apples from the orchards in the fall or peaches and strawberries in the summer. If I am having company, I also make a stop at the liquor store for a nice bottle of wine.

Once I get home with my groceries, I break down my meats into one-meal serving sizes, setting aside some to refrigerate and some to freeze. When you do this, always be sure to mark what the meat is and the date that you have frozen it. You should also use freezer wrap or containers to maintain freshness. Before using any frozen meats, remember to defrost them in the refrigerator the night before. You can also break down your fruits into smaller containers, keeping out any berries that you will be using immediately, and freezing the rest for future use.

If I have the time, I also like to separate and trim any vegetables, and prep them right from my bags (you can also do this on Sunday so you will have them ready for the week to come). Fruits should not be washed before refrigerating. Instead, wash them just before using. Half the work of cooking is the prep work, so if you can cut down on it in advance, it is more likely that you will not bail out on a home-cooked meal and opt for take-out when you are too tired to cook. Salads and vegetable side dishes can also be made ahead, and used throughout the week to save time.

Vary your weekly menu by having meat two to three times each week, along with another protein (like fish, tofu, or a bean-based casserole), and pasta or a vegetarian meal on the other nights. For an easy weekday dinner, prepare a meat pie or quiche that can be frozen, and cut as needed. Making fresh bread and a cake on a Saturday morning will be a treat that you can enjoy for most of the week—if it lasts that long. When making bread, it is often a good idea to double the recipe, because fresh bread has a way of disappearing very quickly.

Of course, if you are having guests or planning a party, your meal preparation will have to be altered—but not by much. You will still be choosing the appetizer, entrée, and dessert to accommodate the amount of people who you will be having. I choose my main course by the type of meat that I will be serving, and then build the rest of my menu around that (although I have been known to be really daring and plan an entire meal around chili pepper season, as well).

I always have a seasonal theme for even small dinner parties or brunches. I sometimes even like to do this for dinners at home with just my son and myself. Matching colors, flowers, and tableware make a lovely meal even more enjoyable. As you work on choosing the meal that you will be making for your guests, also keep in mind any allergies or dietary restrictions that your guests may have. Are they vegans; do they only eat gluten-free meals; do any of your guests have a nut allergy?

There is no wrong way to plan a meal. There is also no wrong dessert. Cupcakes are a handy option: simply pick one up and peel back the paper. Stick to a dessert that matches your main course, and your guests will be thrilled with the selection. After that, you are ready to go.

Organizing a Potluck or Large Dinner

If you are having a large group of people over for a potluck, the planning takes on a new dimension. Along with your appetizers and entrées, serve a big salad with dressing and a variety of homemade breads and butter—and don't forget about dessert. Below are some additional tips for organizing a potluck:

- Start by determining the number of people coming to your potluck. Will it be all adults, or will there be children, as well?

- Assign each guest a dish to bring, specifying the course (for example, appetizer, entrée, or dessert). Keep a list of each dish promised so you do not have duplicates of the same dish.

- Ask your guests to bring their covered dishes cooked in advance and ready to eat. For example, if someone brings a dish using chicken with bones, it should be cut into smaller serving sizes. Meats should be sliced into thin, easy-to-eat slices.

- The individual potluck dishes do not need to be enough to feed the entire party, because guests will sample a bit of each offering.

- If you know that any of your guests have a food allergy, you can either mention it to others who are bringing food or mark the offending dish once it has arrived for the safety of that particular guest.

- As the host/hostess, have ready all serving spoons, platters, bowls, and bread baskets in case they are needed. I find that having one or two hot plates on hand is also prudent.

- Before the potluck, inspect your dinnerware, glasses, and silverware for any chips.

- Be sure to have enough dinnerware to accommodate everyone.

- Arrange the buffet table with plates on one end, and the main dishes and accompaniments set out in the order that you would like your guests to take them (for example, salads first, then breads, and finally utensils and napkins). A long rectangular table is best, but an oblong or round table is just as good. Just be sure to have enough room for everybody's dish.

- Every guest should have a place to sit while they are eating and, ideally, a tabletop to set their plate on (for most potlucks, though, it is fine to stand and hold your plate). Folding chairs and occasional tables are a good idea.

- Appetizers should be set up in a separate area, such as on the coffee table or counters. This will help keep your main buffet table unencumbered and clean.

- There should be one table designated for desserts. I find most people will bring a dessert even if they have also brought an appetizer. Set out the coffee cups in advance: it not only looks pretty, but also saves you time at the end of the party to continue enjoying the company of your guests.

- Save room in the refrigerator for any desserts containing butter cream, cheesecakes, or carrot cakes with cream cheese icing.

- You should be responsible for providing the beverages, such as water, soft drinks, juices, and coffee. Also, be sure to have plenty of extra ice on hand.

- With regards to alcohol, have your guests B.Y.O.B., which means "Bring Your Own Beer" or "Bring Your Own Beverage." Or, if you prefer to provide the alcoholic beverage for the evening, you can make a signature cocktail for the get-together to serve as guests arrive.

- Arrange to have containers on hand for your guests to take home

a sampling from the dishes that they particularly enjoyed.
- If you would like to be the ultimate host/hostess, have available blank recipe cards for someone who might like to exchange a recipe.

Holiday Cookie Exchange

We are always finding ways to enjoy time with friends and family. One way is to hold a cookie exchange around the holidays when everyone makes their Christmas cookies. Each person (usually about 12 people) brings enough homemade cookies to taste at the gathering, plus enough to share. Each person will go home with a dozen different kinds of cookies in pretty tins and the recipes to make them themselves, which can be made into small booklets tied with ribbon for an extra added touch.

Try including these recipes in your next cookie exchange:
- Tea Time Tessies (page 152)
- Grandma LaCapria's Butter Cookies (page 176)
- Neapolitan Cookies (page 139)
- Mom's Christmas Cookies (page 153)
- Homemade Gingersnaps (page 175)
- Jeannine's Ricotta Cookies (page 143)
- Double Chocolate Chip Cookies (page 144)
- Shaker Cookies (page 174)
- Chocolate Chip Drops (page 154)
- Lemon Ricotta Cookies (page 164)

Bake Sale
- Crescent Pastry (page 147)
- Vegan Cupcakes (page 177)
- Christmas Rum Cakes (page 132)
- Vegetarian Mincemeat Tarts (page 122)
- Old-Fashioned Molasses Cookies (page 161)
- Grammy's Cupcakes (page 156)
- Dominican Brownies (page 162)
- Gluten-Free Cheesecake Bars (page 138)

Holiday Brunch

Appetizers/ Breakfast	Entrées/Sides/ Rolls	Desserts	High Tea
Baked French Toast (page 11), Savory Brunch Ring (page 26), Cinnamon Rolls (page 9)	Pizza Rustica (page 109), Easter Bread Ring (page 21), Bialys with Cream Cheese (page 6), Country Potato Quiche (page 89), Fall Farm Stand Quiche (page 83), Beef Wellington (page 90)	Crumb Cake (page 24), Fantastic Carrot Cake (page 140), Cream Cheese Butter Cookies (page 128)	Lemon Layer Cake (page 167), Blueberry Scones with Mock Clotted Cream and Strawberry Preserves (page 15), Cavier Éclair (page 29), Crustless Cranberry Pie (page 135), Chocolate Cream Puffs (page 173), Almond Meringue Torte with Lemon Curd and Hazelnut (page 75), Mélange of Mini-Quiches (page 66)

Resources

Chef Stavros Kokkosis, Aegean Café (Sayville, NY)
www.sayvilleaegeancafe.com

Christine Gable, Queen of the Quick Meal
www.quickmealhelp.com

Steve and Maria Zenk, Zenk's Prairie Vine Farm
szenk@rswb.coop

Amy Acierno
www.missamy.com

Marlisa Brown, M.S., R.D., C.D.E.,
Gluten-Free, Hassle-Free: A Simple, Sane, Dietician-Approved Program for Eating Your Way Back to Health
Marlisa@wellness.net

Chef Christopher Holt, George Martin: The Original
www.georgemartingroup.com

Pastry Chef Werner Simon, Manhattan Sweets Boutique Bakery
www.ManhattanSweetsBB.com

Harry I. Myers
info@poochkies.com

All unidentified recipes courtesy of Monica Musetti-Carlin, mmmjmc53@aol.com

Helpful Websites

Epicurious
www.epicurious.com

Food Network
www.foodnetwork.com

About Southern Food
www.southernfood.about.com

AllRecipes.com
www.allrecipes.com

Cooks.com
www.cooks.com

Index

Request for Future Submissions

I have enjoyed compiling these recipes and stories, and have shared so many special moments with each of the contributors to this book, as we have compared our cooking techniques and traditions. Whether from your own kitchen or from those of family, friends, neighbors, or colleagues, send your recipes to me at mmmjmc53@ aol.com and document your traditions. There is a story behind every recipe.

Please include your name, e-mail address, city, and state. In addition, restaurants should include their chef's name and restaurant website. No previous writing experience is necessary. Your story should be about 150 words, and recipes should list all ingredients, measurements, and directions.

Thank you,
Monica

About the Authors

Monica Musetti-Carlin holds a degree in liberal arts, and is an award-winning media consultant for a chain of newspapers on Long Island, New York. As a journalist, lecturer, and "foodie" with over thirty years of experience in media, she continues to publish news and feature stories, advertorials, restaurant reviews, recipes, and advertising copywriting, and public relations pieces for such publications as *The New York Times, New York Magazine,* and many New York weeklies. She has had the opportunity to work with Jane Brody, Pete Seeger, and Yoko Ono.

Monica Musetti-Carlin's Eclectic Endeavors, Inc., markets and distributes her recipe and craft products. In addition to writing the *Country Comfort* series, she is completing a work of fiction called *Park Slope.*

Chef Christopher Holt was born and raised in Great Neck, New York. Chef Holt began working at the age of 13 and quickly found his calling in the culinary arts. He joined the George Martin Restaurant Group in 1991 and was promoted to executive chef of George Martin: The Original in 1995. In 2007, George Martin: The Original was awarded the rating of "Excellent" by Joanne Starkey of *The New York Times.* Chef Holt resides in Seaford, New York with his wife Amy and their three children.

Harry I. Myers previously worked as a marketing executive in New York and now lives in Texas. Upon retirement, Harry turned his interests towards baking and cooking the foods he grew up with in Brooklyn, New York because he could no longer find his favorite dishes in his new home state. Finding and recreating New York-style recipes has sustained his joy of keeping those foods close to home.

Also in the *Country Comfort* series...

Country Comfort: Casserole Cooking
ISBN: 978-1-57826-404-9

Country Comfort: Cooking Across America
ISBN: 978-1-57826-414-8

Country Comfort: Harvest
ISBN: 978-1-57826-359-2

Country Comfort: Holidays
ISBN: 978-1-57826-380-6

Country Comfort: Slow-Cooker Favorites
ISBN: 978-1-57826-374-5

Country Comfort: Summer Favorites
ISBN: 978-1-57826-384-4